The Hygiene Of Health And Disease

Herbert M. Shelton

Kessinger Publishing's Rare Reprints

Thousands of Scarce and Hard-to-Find Books on These and other Subjects!

- Americana
- Ancient Mysteries
- Animals
- Anthropology
- Architecture
- Arts
- Astrology
- Bibliographies
- Biographies & Memoirs
- Body, Mind & Spirit
- Business & Investing
- Children & Young Adult
- Collectibles
- Comparative Religions
- Crafts & Hobbies
- Earth Sciences
- Education
- Ephemera
- Fiction
- Folklore
- Geography
- Health & Diet
- History
- Hobbies & Leisure
- Humor
- Illustrated Books
- Language & Culture
- Law
- Life Sciences
- Literature
- Medicine & Pharmacy
- Metaphysical
- Music
- Mystery & Crime
- Mythology
- Natural History
- Outdoor & Nature
- Philosophy
- Poetry
- Political Science
- Science
- Psychiatry & Psychology
- Reference
- Religion & Spiritualism
- Rhetoric
- Sacred Books
- Science Fiction
- Science & Technology
- Self-Help
- Social Sciences
- Symbolism
- Theatre & Drama
- Theology
- Travel & Explorations
- War & Military
- Women
- Yoga
- *Plus Much More!*

We kindly invite you to view our catalog list at:
http://www.kessinger.net

THIS ARTICLE WAS EXTRACTED FROM THE BOOK:

Human Life Its Philosophy and Laws: An Exposition of the Principles and Practices of Orthopathy

BY THIS AUTHOR:

Herbert M. Shelton

ISBN 1564597148

READ MORE ABOUT THE BOOK AT OUR WEB SITE:

http://www.kessinger.net

OR ORDER THE COMPLETE
BOOK FROM YOUR FAVORITE STORE

ISBN 1564597148

Because this article has been extracted from a parent book, it may have non-pertinent text at the beginning or end of it.

Any blank pages following the article are necessary for our book production requirements. The article herein is complete.

THE HYGIENE OF HEALTH
CHAPTER XXVIII

HYGIENE is that branch of biology that relates to the preservation and restoration of health. Bionomy is the science of the laws of living functions; or that branch of biology which treats of habits and adaptation. Orthobionomics is a word I have coined to designate the correct adaptation of life and environment to each other.

The hygiene of health and the hygiene of disease is one. However, for convenience, we divide it into *Preventive Hygiene*, or the *hygiene of healthful maintenance*, and *Remedial Hygiene*, or the *hygiene of health restoration*.

By *Preventive Hygiene* is meant the intelligent employment of hygienic principles, forces and agencies for the maintenance of functional and structural integrity.

By *Remedial Hygiene* is understood the intelligent employment of hygienic principles, forces and agencies for the restoration of sound health.

"There must be a way to live exactly right, which, if a man does, he will grow into health," said a young school-teacher to himself some years ago. He was beginning to despair of his life because every doctor to whom he went diagnosed his case differently and proceeded to make him much worse than ever. Then began a long series of experiments upon his own body, and years of study of the subjects that relate to health and disease. That man, young Robert Walter, later became one of the leaders in the nature cure or hygienic movement. Like many others who have turned to hygiene he was forced to study the matter out for himself because physicians are interested in disease and not in living.

A soap-box lecturer was once entertaining a crowd on Broadway in New York City. He told the following story:—

"The superintendent of an institution for the feeble-minded sent an inmate into the basement to mop up the water from a faucet that accidently had been left running. Later in the day the man was found mopping with the water still running full blast. 'You darned idiot, why don't you turn off the faucet,' shouted the superintendent. The simpleton grinned and replied: 'Nobody's paying me to turn 'er off. I'm gettin two bits an hour to mop 'er up.'"

When the roar that greeted this jibe at the medical profession had subsided, the speaker continued: "The land is flooded with sickness which flows from ignorance of nature's laws. Proper instruction would shut off disease at its source, but if doctors turned off the tap, they would put themselves out of a job."

Nobody pays the medical profession to "turn 'er off," they get "two bits an hour to mop 'er up."

Physiology, alone, can teach us how man must live in order to secure the best health and attain to the greatest age of which the human constitution is capable. The fact that there are individuals now living a hundred years old, proves that the human constitution is capable of sustaining life a hundred years at least, and perhaps much longer, if the mode of life is, in all respects, correct. Here we shall probably be met with the very ancient and utterly absurd doctrine, that there are different constitutions, and therefore, that what may be true of one, cannot truly be affirmed of all. What is one man's elixir is another man's bane. We freely admit that, in the present state of mankind, some individuals have more vital energy and constitutional power to resist the causes of disease and death than others have, and therefore, what will break down the constitution and destroy the life of some individuals, may be borne by others a much longer time without any striking manifestations of immediate injury. Some can withstand more abuse than others. It is also true that, in the present state of man, some individuals have strongly marked idiosyncrasies or peculiarities; but these are far more rare and of a much less important character than is generally supposed, and in no instance do they constitute the slightest exception to the general laws of life, nor in any degree interfere with, or militate against, the correct principles of a general regimen. Indeed, such peculiarities, though really constitutional, may in almost every case be overcome entirely by a correct regime. "I have frequently," says Graham, "seen the most strongly marked cases completely subdued by such means. It is an incontrovertible truth, therefore, that so far as the general laws of life and the application of the general principles of regimen are considered, the human constitution is ONE; and there are no constitutional differences in the human race which will not readily yield to a correct regimen, and by thus yielding improve the condition of the individual affected; and consequently, there are no constitutional differences in the human race which stand in the way of adopting one general regimen to the whole family of man; but, on the contrary, it is most strictly true that, so far as the general laws of life and the application of general principles of regimen are considered, what may be truly affirmed of one man may be truly affirmed of all, and what is best for one is best for all; and therefore, all general reasonings concerning the human constitution, are equally applicable to each and every member of the human family, in all ages of the world, and in all conditions of the race, and in all the various circumstances of the individual."

All of which simply means that what is truly a healthful life for Mr. Smith is equally healthful for Mr. Jones. But it does not follow that because Smith, with a much more powerful constitution than Jones, resists the influence of a disease building regimen longer than Jones, that what is Smith's meat is Jones' poison. It only shows that due to the differences in their constitutional strength, not to any differences in their constitutional nature, it requires more poison to kill Smith than to kill Jones. But the essential point which Mr. Graham, and so far as we are aware, all subsequent writers on this subject, overlooked is that, we are not trying to fit an unhealthful regime to Jones and get him to live as long as Smith under the same unhealthful regime; but we are attempting to fit a regime that is essentially healthful to all—we would remove, as far as possible, the causes of disease that the constitutional powers of both men are forced to resist. We seek to accomplish this in a strictly natural way for as Graham pointed out, artificial means are all harmful.

It would be impossible for two men with equally excellent constitutions, to reach an equally advanced age, with habits of life exactly opposite, without a very marked and apparent difference in condition and appearance of both body and mind. *It is not possible for two men of equally excellent constitutions to start out in life and follow such equally opposite courses and arrive at the same goal.*

That a life just lived as it happened, filled with numerous and various excesses, would enable a man to reach the hundred mark in as good mental and physical condition as another would be in, at the same age, who had led a temperate and well ordered life, is absurd on the face of it. To believe such is to believe that life is subject to no law, that man is at the mercy of fortuitous circumstances or a capricious Providence; that hygiene and sanitation are valueless, inebriety is as good as temperance, gluttony as salubrious as moderation, sensuality as healthful as virtue, impurity and nastiness as beneficial as purity and cleanliness, chaos as approved as order. Are we to believe that there are no rules of health—no laws governing life? Or, are we to believe that, if such laws do exist, they are not binding, and that we may voluntarily set them aside when we will? Are the laws governing health any less real than those governing mathematics or chemistry. Do acts have no consequences in the realm of life?

Anyone, with common intelligence, can readily discern that, if health and rigid hygiene do not prevent disease, then, man is left a helpless victim of chance, a ready prey to the "devouring monsters," and must remain so until he discovers some effective barrier against the inroads of germs and worse. If a body pulsating with vitality and full of pure blood, is no guarantee against disease, so long, as, by hygienic living, it is maintained in this state, then health and hygiene are failures and man is indeed the helpless victim of circumstances beyond his control. If he possesses good health, it is simply due to his good fortune and not to his good behavior.

Those who hold to such a doctrine may laugh at the laws of life, and violate them continually, and, then if they possess a sound, vigorous constitution, they may abuse themselves a long time before the effects of those abuses show. But none but the fool can believe that even the most rugged constitution can be abused indefinitely without hurt.

THE HYGIENE OF HEALTH

In the preceding chapters the following facts have been shown:—

1. By virtue of the body's inherent and automatic powers of self-renewal, self-renovation and self-regeneration and its undeviating tendency to fullness of life, it is capable of a much longer existence and a much higher existence than men and women now live.

2. Disease, degeneracy and death come as the immediate result of poisoning and starvation of the cells of the body, as a consequence of a combination of forces and influences which are largely under individual control and usually self-inflicted.

These facts serve to confirm the old statement that "man does not die; he kills himself." Men and women are dying far short of the age they are capable of attaining because they are engaged in committing slow suicide.

Given a normal organism, at birth, and a proper mode of living afterward, together with absence from injurious influences, and every baby born into this world will grow into a strong, healthy man or woman. Those same simple conditions that are the sources of the development of plant, animal and man from germ to maturity are the constant sources of the maintenance of these organisms after maturity is reached. Those same influences that impair or prevent development in the growing child or youth also impair the powers of life in adults.

Whether you have a good organism at birth will depend partly upon heredity and partly upon the nutrition you received from your mother. What that organism will become after birth, that is, whether it will reach up to its highest potentiality, or fall far short of its inherent possibilities, will depend upon how you live. Of course there will be social factors that are not subject to individual control that may mar your life to a certain extent, but for the most part you and your parents and teachers will determine your life.

You cannot change your heredity. You cannot change your past. You cannot make society over. But you can work for the betterment of these things for the future. Civilization has many influences in it that are inimical to health and life. But these are not inherent in it and may be eradicated. We can build for a better future and assure our children and grandchildren better conditions to grow up under. The standard of living can be raised; the conditions of life can be improved not merely for the fortunate few, but for all.

So prone is man to look upon the conditions under which he is born and reared as natural and to look upon those things which the majority of mankind do as an average as the best for us to do as a whole that few are inclined to question the wisdom of the conventional standards of health and living, with a view to ascertaining if these best serve the physiological and psychological welfare of the individual and the race, but take it for granted that they do so. There is a happy delusion, a very convenient substitute for thought, that our present customs and standards represent the boiled down results of thousands of years of race experience and that they should not be tampered with. If it can be shown, historically, that a particular custom is old, this suffices to establish its value in the minds of many. Nothing could be farther from the truth.

Laboring under the delusions above noted, the physician or health advisor who insists that his patients abandon certain of their pet vices and health destroying practices and indulgences, is justly considered severe. The practitioner, however, if he is to be held responsible for the health and life of his patient, must necessarily be firm and insist upon obedience to natural law. The laws of nature are sharply defined, their penalties inexorable, if not always swift, and as an interpreter of her decrees, the hygienist, under present thought, at least, cannot seem otherwise than severe. However, it is not the hygienist but nature that is severe. This being true, it behooves the health seeker to strive to understand God's rational order, that he may render an intelligent obedience to laws which cannot be broken, but, upon which, we only break ourselves, in the attempt.

When we come to consider the means best suited to maintain life and health, youth, strength and beauty, it is obvious that THE HIGHEST POSSIBLE STANDARD MUST BE ACCEPTED. How, then shall we live?

1. CULTIVATE POISE AND CHEER. Do not attempt to see the world through the rose-colored glasses of a sentimental Pollyana but learn to take joy and

sorrow, good fortune and misfortune with the same calmness and equitableness. Avoid worry, fear, anxiety, excitement, jealousy, anger, self-pity, etc. Control your temper, passions, and emotions.

2. EXERCISE DAILY. Daily physical exercise, preferably in the fresh air and sunshine, and, as often as possible, in the form of play, is essential to both mental and physical health. Avoid the strenuous life, however. Do not make the Rooseveltian mistake and imagine that a strenuous physical life can offset gluttony.

3. SECURE PLENTY OF REST AND SLEEP EACH DAY: Learn to retire early. Learn to relax and "let go." Earn your sleep by honest work and avoid stimulants and sleep will come easily and naturally. Do not turn the night into day. Time is never wasted that is spent in recuperation.

Sleep may be defined as the periodical suspension of all the functions of external relation. Profound or quiet sleep is the complete suspension of the functions of the mind and special senses and is attended with entire unconsciousness. Normal sleep is dreamless. Dreaming implies imperfect rest. In default of this oblivion, sleep is only partial. It is not perfect nervous repose. It indicates some disturbing cause, some source of irritation and worry, such as gastric irritation. No person who suffers severly from indigestion but is also troubled with much dreaming, and, more or less, wakefulness. Irritants, stimulants, fear, apprehension, worry, grief, etc., interfere with sleep and prevent prefect repose, rest, recuperation.

The amount of sleep required will vary with the varying habits and occupations of individuals. Those who are the most active will require most sleep. Meat eaters, as in the animal kingdom, require more sleep than vegetarians. Mental workers require more sleep than physical workers. Those who dissipate much must sleep much. The sick require more sleep than the well. The accepted rule of eight hours in twenty-four is probably not enough, for as Trall says: "The statute of nature appears to read: Retire soon after dark, and arise with the first rays of morning light; and this is equally applicable to all climates and all seasons, at least in all parts of the globe proper for human habitation, for in the cold season, when the nights are longer, more sleep is required." When man learned to turn the night into day he forsook this natural rule.

4. KEEP CLEAN: This refers to both body and mind. Keep clean clothes, clean beds, clean houses. Keep the mind clean. Avoid lustful thoughts and desires. Do not become covetous, deceitful or corrupt. Nature penalizes you for all these things with hardening of the arteries and a shortened life.

Keep your body clean but do not indulge in too frequent and prolonged bathing. Do not soak yourself. Keep in mind that man is neither fish nor amphibian. He is a land mammal and his body was originally self-cleansing. Bathing is an artificial proceedure made necessary by clothing and civilization. Trall says: "Were human beings in all other respects to adapt themselves to the laws of their organization, and were they in all their voluntary habits in relation to eating, drinking, clothing, exercise, and temperature, to conform strictly to the laws of hygiene, I do not know that there would be any physiological necessity or utility in bathing at all." Page agrees with this saying: "The less clothing one wears, the less essential a daily bath becomes, and the less time necessary to devote to it. At the same time there is an increased ability to withstand exposure to wet or cold, whether of the bath, an involuntary ducking, or however caused."

A daily friction bath is sufficient for many. No one except those who sweat much or who work in occupations that make them dirty, requires a daily water bath. In these cases the water should be lukewarm or slightly cool. Hot and cold bathing should be avoided. Unless the nature of the "dirt" on the body demands soap for its removal, this is best avoided. Soap should form no part of the average bath.

5. BREATHE FRESH PURE AIR: Keep your windows open. Have your living room, bed room, office or workshop well ventilated. Get out of doors as much as possible. If you live in the city take advantage of every opportunity to get into the country.

6. SECURE AS MUCH SUNSHINE AS POSSIBLE: This means that your nude body, or as much of it as circumstances will permit, should be exposed to the direct rays of the sun. To merely sit by the window, or take a walk in the sunshine heavily clad, or clad in dark clothing will be of no benefit in so far as the sunshine is

concerned. Get your sun-baths in the morning or evening when it is not excessively hot.

7. EAT MODERATELY OF WHOLESOME FOODS: What are wholesome foods? All true foods that are fresh, pure, unadulterated and that have not been processed, refined, and cooked until their food value is largely destroyed, are wholesome foods. All foods that, in the process of refining, manufacturing, pickling, canning, preserving, and cooking, etc., have been deprived of their mineral elements and vitamins or that have been adulterated and poisoned by bleaching, coloring, flavoring, seasoning and by preservatives, are more or less unwholesome. All foods that have been raised in defective soil, hot houses, or on manure-fed lands or on lands fed with packing-house fertilizers, or that are raised out of the sunlight, are more or less unwholesome. All foods that have begun to undergo decomposition are unwholesome.

Man may eat unwholesome foods all his life, thanks to his wonderful powers of self-immunization and adaptation, and enjoy what ordinarily passes for health. "Excess in moderately unwholesome viands," says Oswald, "has to be carried to a monstrous degree before the after-dinner torpor turns into a malignant disease; the stomach**** seems to acquire a knack of assimilating a modicum of the ingesta and voiding the rest like so much unnutritious stuff."

However, the rule that applies to unnatural habits in general also applies, and very forcibly, to chronic dietetic abuses—namely: The further we have strayed from nature the longer, wearier and more painful will be the road to reform. Dr. Oswald paints a vivid pen picture of the trials of the dyspeptics in his *Household Remedies*, p. 54-58.

"To the alcholic stimulants of the ancients we have added tea, coffee, tobacco, absinthe, chloral, opium, and pungent spices. Every year increases the number of our elaborately unwholesome-made dishes, and decreases our devotion to the field-sports that helped our forefathers to digest their boar-steaks. We have no time to masticate our food; we bolt it, and grumble if we can not bolt it smoking hot. The competition of our domestic and public kitchens temps us to eat three full meals a day, and two of them at a time when the exigencies of our business-routine leave us no leisure for digestion. At night, when the opportunity for that leisure arrives, we counteract the efforts of the digestive apparatus by hot stove-fires and stifling bedrooms. Since the beginning of the commercial-epicurean age of the nineteenth century the votaries of fashion have persistently vied in compelling their stomachs to dispose of the largest possible amount of the most indigestible food under the least favorable circumstances.

"That persistence has at last exhausted the self-regulating resources of our digestive organs. But even after such provocations the stomach does not strike work without repeated warnings. The first omen of the wrath to come is the *morning languor*, the hollow-eyed lassitude which proves that the arduous labor of the assimilative organs has made the night the most fatiguing part of the twenty-four hours. The expression of the face becomes haggard and sallow. The tongue feels gritty, the palate parched, in spite of the restless activity of the salivary glands, which every now and then try to respond to the appeals of the distressed stomach. Gastric acidity betrays itself by many disagreeable symptoms; loss of appetite, however, marks a later stage of the malady. For years the infinite patience of Nature labors every night to undo the mischief of every day, and before noon the surfeited organs again report ready for duty. Habitual excess in eating and drinking sometimes begets an unnatural appetency that enables the glutten to indulge his *penchant* to the last, only with this difference, that the relish for special kinds of food has changed into a vague craving for *repletion*, just as the fondness for a special stimulant is apt to turn into a chronic poison-hunger. This craving after engorgement forms a distinctive symptom of *plethoric dyspepsia*, but even in the first stage of asthenic or nervous dyspepsia the hankering after food is not hunger proper, but a nervous uneasiness, suggesting the idea that a good meal would, somehow supply the means of relief. The first full meal, however, entails penalties which the sufferer would gladly exchange for the less positive discomfort of the morning. Instinct fails to keep its promise, as a proof that Nature has been supplanted by a deceptive second nature. Headache, heart-burn, eructations, humming in the ears, nausea, vertigo, and gastric spasms, make the after-dinner hour "the saddest of the sad twenty-four!": a dull mist of discontent broods over the whole afternoon, and yields only to tea and lamp-light. The patient begins to fret under the weight of his affliction, but still declines to remove the cause. To out-door exercise he objects, not on general principles, but on some special plea or other. He has to husband his strength. The raw March wind would turn his cough into a chronic catarrh. The warm weather would spoil his appetite and aggravate his vertigo. The truth is that of the large quantum of comestibles ingested only a small modicum is *digested*, and that the system begins to weaken under the influence of indirect starvation. Business routine prevents the dyspeptic from changing his meal times. He cannot reduce the number of his meals; people have to conform to the arrangements of their boarding-house. The stomach needs something strengthening between breakfast and supper. The truth is, that the exertions of the digestive organs alternate with occasional reactions, entailing a nervous depression which can be (temporarily) relieved by the stimulus of a fresh engorgement. Business reasons may really prevent a reduction of working hours, and domestic duties a change of climate or of occupation. The daily engorgement in the meanwhile goes on as before.

"Nature then resorts to more emphatic protests. Sleep comes in the form of a dull torpor that would make a nightmare a pleasant change of programme. The digestive laboratory seems to have lost the discretion of its automatic contrivances; the process of assimilation, in all its details, obtrudes itself upon the cognizance of the sensorium, and urges the co-operation of the voluntary muscles. Contortions and pressing manipulations have to force each morsel through the gastric apparatus; the lining of the stomach has become sentient, and shirks its work like a blistered palate. Special tidbits can be traced through the whole course of their abdominal adventures. Undigested green peas roll on like buckshot shot from the smelting-pan of a shot-tower. A grilled partridge crawls along like a reluctant crab, clawing and biting at each step. Nausea and headache strive to relieve themselves in spasmodic eructations. Vertigoes, like fainting-fits, eclipse the eyesight for minutes together. Constipation, often combined with a morbid appetite, suggests distressful speculations on the possible outcome of the accumulating ingesta. The overfed organism is under-nourished to a degree that reveals itself in the rapid emaciation of the patient. The general derangement of the nervous system reacts on the mental faculties, and impairs their efficacy even for the most ordinary business purposes, till the invalid at last realizes the necessity of reform. He tries to reduce the number of his meals; but the lengthened intervals drag as heavily as the toper's time between drinks. He hopes to appease his stomach by a change of diet, but finds that the resolution has come too late; the gastric mutiny has become indiscriminate, and protests as savagely against a Graham biscuit as against a broiled pork sausage. He tries pedestrianism, but finds the remedy worse than the evil. The enemy has cut off his means of retreat; the necessitous system has no strength to spare for such purposes as an effort of the motive organs. But nine out of ten dyspeptics resort to the drug-store. They get a bottle of "tonic bitters." They try Dr. Quack's 'Dysepepsia Elixir.' They try a 'blue pill'—in the hope of rousing Nature, as it were, to a sense of her proper duty.

"Now, what such 'tonics' can really do for them is this: they goad the system into the transient and abnormal activity incident to the necessity of expelling a virulent poison. With the accomplishment of that purpose the exertion ceases, and the ensuing exhaustion is worse than the first by just as much as the *poison-fever* has robbed the system of a larger or smaller share of its little remaining strength. The stimulant has wasted the organic energy which it seemed to revive."

8. BE MODERATE IN WEARING CLOTHES: It may be stated that, as a general rule, the less clothes one wears the healthier he will be. The materials should be light, porous and white or of light colors. Dark or black clothing should be avoided like snakes. No tight bands, belts, corsets, garters, etc., should be allowed to interfere with the circulation nor cramp up the organs of the body. Shoe heels shauld be absent or, at most, very low. Shoes should fit the feet and the feet not made to fit the shoes. Some day sandals and a string of beads will be our chief articles of clothing.

We may present the case for and against clothes in the words of Graham, *Science of Human Life*, p. 637-9:—

"It is entirely certain that no kind of clothing is strictly natural to man;*** all the physiological and psychological properties, powers, and interests of the human constitution would be better sustained, as a permanent fact, from generation to generation, by entire nudity, than by the use of any kind of clothing. Strictly speaking, therefore, all clothing is, in itself considered, in some measure an evil. In passing into climates much cooler than that to which he is constitutionally adapted, however, man finds it necessary to employ clothing to a greater or less extent, for the purpose of preserving the proper temperature of his body. In such a situation therefore, clothing becomes a *necessary evil;* and in so far as man suffers cold without it, it is a comparative good; that is, it prevents a greater evil than it causes. Nevertheless it cannot serve to adapt man so perfectly to such a situation as to make it equally conductive to the highest well being of the human constitution with his natural climate without clothing, it remains true, as a general proposition, that clothing is in some measure detrimental to the physiological interests of the human body.**** Clothing, then, is an evil so far as it prevents a free circulation of pure air over the whole surface of the body, or in any manner relaxes and debilitates the skin; and increases its susceptibility to be unhealthily affected by changes of weather and by the action of morbific agents; it is an evil in as far as, by compression or otherwise, it prevents the free action of the chest and lungs, or in any manner or measure restricts respiration; it is an evil in so far as it interferes in any degree with the digestive organs; it is an evil so far as it prevents the most perfect freedom of voluntary action, and ease and grace of motion and attitude, or prevents the full development of any part of the system, or serves, by the substitution of artificial means for natural powers, to relax and debilitate the muscles, or render the tendons, ligaments, cartilages, and boxes, less healthy and powerful, or in any measure to abridge the control of the will over any organ of voluntary motion; it is an evil in so far as it tends to increase the peculiar sensibility of any organ of animal instinct, and to augment the power of that instinct on the intellectual and moral faculties; it is an evil so far as it serves to enfeeble the intellectual faculties, and render the mind sluggish and sensual; and it is an evil so far as it serves to excite an unchaste imagination, and cause the sexes to act towards each other more from the impulse of animal feeling than from the dictate of sound reason."

Mr Graham quotes one Rev. Grout as saying in 1168:—

"The Zulus depend on the products of the soil for subsistence, and go entirely naked. Licentiousness is wholly unknown among them. I have been among them for three years, seen them on all occasions, have many a time seen hundreds of males and females huddled together in perfect nakedness, but never once saw the least manifestation of licentious feeling, and they are as remarkable for their intellectual activity and aptitude as for their chastity."

This is the general testimony of missionaries, explorers and scientists and accords with just what we should, on general principles, expect. Prudery and shame for the body came after and not before man began to wear clothes.

Man will not be ready to discard clothes for at least another decade and in the meantime he should clothe himself as lightly and sensibly as possible. Overclothing weakens the body. It lowers resistance to heat and cold and impairs the power of adaptation to weather changes. It deprives the body of the sun and air and keeps the excretions of the skin locked up against the body. You are literally wallowing in your own excretions.

9. HAVE AN INTEREST IN LIFE: A purposeless life is marked for early dissolution. A purposeless life is not worthy of preservation. That man or woman who has no purpose in life is driven about from place to place; from discontent to despair.

10. GET MARRIED: Build a home. Rear a family. Statistics show that married people live longer on the average than single people.

Dr. George Robertson of the Edinburgh Royal College of Physicians recently stated that "Young men between 25 and 35 who remain bachelors die four years sooner than married men." He added that they also "Run three times the risk of becoming insane." It is not, of course, fair to charge all this apparent evil of "single blessedness" to the single life. We can only correctly interpret such figures when we understand why these men remained single. All normal, healthy men marry, or, at least, desire to.

It is safe to assume that a great majority of those who remain single from choice are lacking in virility and are diseased perhaps in many ways. The thing that prevented them from marrying may also have been the thing that caused their early death or that caused so much insanity among them. *Statistics give results, not causes.*

Childless couples die before those with children. A childless marriage is usually more unhappy than where there are children. Home and children stabilize life.

Avoid contraceptives of all kinds. They are all harmful and all lead to sex glutteny. They are partly responsible for so much cancer of the womb in women. Don't build your married life on lust.

11. AVOID ALL POISON HABITS: Coffee, tea, cocoa, chocolate, tobacco, alcohol, opium, heroin, soda fountain slops and other drugs. These all weaken, poison and destroy the body.

12. AVOID SEXUAL EXCESS: All sexual relations,—"petting," mental self-abuse, self-abuse and all indulgences—drain the nervous system of much of its powers. Conserve these powers.

13. AVOID ALL EXCESSES: Build your life on the conservation of energy, not upon its dissipation. Don't waste your forces in useless and needless expenditures. Be moderate and temperate in all things. If you waste your forces you impair your functions and build toxemia and impaired nutrition.

We are living in an age of thrills and excitement. These things have been commercialized and organized on a large scale. They are habit-forming and progressive in their tendency. They build a very unstable nervous system and wreck one's health. Life without some thrill and excitement would be monotonous, but the pursuit of these things as an end in itself is an unmitigated evil. One invariably goes to excess and as satiety is derived from one form, craves and seeks a more thrilling and more exciting form.

14. DO NOT BECOME ONE-SIDED IN YOUR MANNER OF LIVING: You cannot remain or become well and strong through exercise alone, or through diet alone, or rest and sleep alone. Fresh air and sunshine alone are not enough. Do not imagine that by breathing alone you can reach the heights. All these things are good, but life is more than exercise, or food and drink; more than thought, or rest and sleep. It is all these and more. Life must be lived as a whole.

Do not get the idea that you are an exception to laws of life. There are no exceptions. The laws that govern life, health, growth, development, disease and death in your body are the same laws that govern these same processes in the bodies of your neighbors. Physiological laws and processes are the same in Jones as in Smith. Both Jones and his neighbors are injured by the same harmful indulgencies, practices, habits, agents and influences. Both are helped by the same factors. Paste this in your hat. YOU ARE NO EXCEPTION.

We must learn to view life as a struggle between self-control and self-indulgence and must come to realize that self-control alone leads to strength and happiness. Self-indulgence leads to misery and destruction. The late Eblert Hubbard well said: "The rewards of life are for service, its penalties for self-indulgence."

There is absolutely no need for any action or habit that impairs life and produces weakness and disease. But people are so enslaved by their habits, so bent on the pleasures of the moment, so lacking in self-control that they cannot free themselves. Self-control is the world's greatest need. Self-discipline is the only saving force. Our pleasure-mad and over-stimulated age is almost wholly lacking in self-control.

Many will say: "I would rather live as I now do and only live ten years than to live as you have outlined and live a hundred." They do not realize that this is the despairing cry of a slave. These people are hopelessly enslaved by their bad habits and thoroughly perverted in both mind and body. Mind and body alike are dominated by their habits. They are beyond redemption. They will declare they derive more satisfaction from their pipe or cigar than from anything else in life. Or they cry out. "Please don't take my harem away." It is but a waste of time to reason with such. One is always defeated in an argument with their appetites and morbid desires and perverted instincts.

THE HYGIENE OF HEALTH

Their cry is "We live but once. Let us enjoy life while we are here." We believe in enjoying life, real life, life in the highest and fullest sense, not life on the low groveling plane they mean. What they should say is: "We live but once, let us make it short and snappy."

If these people would only die at the end of their ten fast and merry years, little objection could be offered to their foolish "philosophy" and worse practices. But many of them do not do this. Instead, they hang on year after year, going from doctor to doctor and from institution to institution in search of a cure for the effects of the very abuses of their bodies from which they think they derive so much pleasure and satisfaction. They desire to be SAVED IN THEIR SINS—not FROM THEM. The "*satisfaction*" they derive from their pipe, or their glutteny or their alcohol or from their harem is a poor satisfaction. It is a poor substitute for the higher joys of real health based on wholesome living. If you would live longer; live simply, live wholesomely, live right.

A few words anent the hygiene of pregnancy and the hygiene of infancy are required before we close this chapter.

Pregnancy is a strictly normal, natural condition, it is not a disease, and those abnormal symptoms that are usually listed as symptoms of pregnancy are not symptoms of pregnancy at all. Likewise, when pregnancy is given as a cause or a predisposing cause of disease those who give it do so either ignorantly or thoughtlessly. Pregnancy actually serves to benefit the body and many women have lost their ills through this alone.

Live a normal life as outlined above and pregnancy will take care of itself. Throw away all foolish fears of marking your baby. This is an impossible thing, a mere superstition. Avoid all sexual relations during this period and during lactation.

Parturition is not a surgical operation. It is not a wound, accident, infection or other abnormal condition. If you have lived as you should and were normal at the beginning of pregnancy, an easy, sometimes painless and rapid delivery will be experienced and a rapid recuperation follow. There will be no necessity for remaining on your back for days, as is the common practice.

Babies should be nursed at their mother's breast, whenever possible for as long as possible. Three to four years should be the normal length of the period of lactation, and not four to five weeks as one so often sees today.

Babies should be fed as directed in the chapter on diet. They should be kept clean, let alone as much as possible and dressed lightly, if at all. A daily sun-bath should be given them. Even Dr. Tilden, who objects to the sun-bath for the almost childish reason (or vanity) that he does not want his skin brown like a Mexican, but prefers it pale like a corpse, advocates sun-baths for infants and children.

Babies should be placed on their stomachs from the day of birth. In this way they develop their backs, necks, arms and legs much more rapidly than when lying on their back. This is Dr. Page's method and is the best exercise of which I know for infants.

Place them on a hard bed, give them plenty of fresh air, do not bundle them up, keep stays, swaddling bands, caps, etc., off of them and give them a chance to kick and grow. Never put flannels on a child. Cotton, linen or silk will answer far better. Nudity is better still.

Do not be afraid that they will "Catch Cold." A child that is properly cared for could no more have a cold than it could fly. You could freeze it to death, but you could not cause it to have a cold by exposure. Do not think from this, however, that you should expose the child unduly. Forget the old superstitions about night air.

THE HYGIENE OF ACUTE DISEASE
Chapter XXIX

WE are suffering from a frightful incubus of so-called science that murders millions with its almost incredible ignorance. For "Medical Science" we have a "science" which is fighting nature with every resource at its command. Science is the knowledge of a body of ascertained facts (ascertained by observation and subsequent demonstration), and their causes, organized and classified according to their natural relationships. The terms "science" and "scientific" are employed today in such a loose, haphazzard and indiscriminate manner, and people have become so thoroughly hypnotized by the term, that it becomes frequently necessary to discuss the question, "what is science?" Medicine is not, was never, and can never be, a science. When the problems of health, disease and living have been reduced to a science, medicine will quickly cease to exist.

When the essential nature and purpose, the rationale, of acute disease is fully understood, it will no longer be treated. Its symptoms will no longer be suppressed, subdued, changed, or combatted. To again quote Jennings:—

"The vital economy has but one great and absorbing object before it and in the prosecution of that object, it is not easily diverted to the right hand or to the left. When difficulties thicken in its pathway, its forces are all put in requisition, disposed and used to the best advantage for surmounting the difficulties, and it is instructive as well as astonishing to witness the amount of obstacles that human nature will often overcome and still hold on her way, even under apparently, an almost exhausted state of the vital energies."—*Philosophy of Human Life*, p. 219.

The Orthopath is legitimately absolved from all warfare against "disease." For in his view there is nothing against which to battle. For as Dr. Jennings declares:—

"For the recovery of his charge he looks to the operation of internal vital machinery most perfectly adapted to the purpose,—and controlled by laws that need and admit of no improvement. While faithfully serving in the capacity of handmaid to nature, in the arrangement and constant adaptation of external circumstances to the natural renovating efforts, he expects occasionally to witness fearful and agonizing convulsions and disturbances of the motory portions of the vital mechanism, or great deviation of some kind from the natural state. But instead of regarding these changes and these irregular actions as subversive in their nature and tendency, he considers them as directly the opposite of this, and as truly essential to the reparation and replenishment of a damaged living body, as thunder storms are for the purification of the atmosphere. And a principal source of his anxiety and vigilance is to guard the delicate nervous, apparatus whose function is to transmit intelligence and power, and control motion— from the presence and action of anything that has a tendency to impair its perceptive faculty, agileness and force.

"It is immaterial, therefore, to the Orthopathist, so far as his direct interference is concerned in what shape disease makes its appearance, and with what severity; or what changes it undergoes. His business is to guard and take proper care of the exterior of the body, furnish a little 'bread and water' as it may be called for, secure a quiet and equable state of mind, and leave nature full scope and freedom in the discharge of her own appropriate duties. If death should peer forth in pale and ghastly visage, and show its icy hand as if to clutch away the remnant of humanity, it would be out of order for our Orthopathist to attempt to repel it by the employment of any of the troops of Admiral Mercury, King Alcohol, General Diffusive Stimuli, Subordinate or Local Irritants, or any other contraband force. He should fall back submissively upon the extreme resources of nature, as his *dernier* resort, and if these fail, the final catastrophe is sealed."—*Philosophy of Human Life*, p. 267.

The Orthopathic practice is a let-alone practice. Prof. O. S. Fowler declared: "The Let-Alone Cure is but the outgrowth of the Will-Cure. How many millions have grown worse by doctoring till they had no more means or hope, given up, did nothing, waited to die, (in these cases not *willing* to get well. Author's note.) kept on living to their wonderment, and finally got well. What a pity! Not their getting well, but keeping themselves sick so long by so expensive a practice."

THE HYGIENE OF ACUTE DISEASE

Orthopathy recognizes no therapeutics of acute disease. It only recognizes the hygiene of acute disease. Seeing in the acute process the PROCESS OF CURE, it does not seek to cure disease, CURE THE CURE, but seeks merely to supply the body with the best hygienic conditions to the end that it may carry forward its curative work with the least possible hinderance. Knowing no power of cure except that inherent in living matter, orthopathy does not seek for curative agencies and influencies outside the body. Knowing that every action of the living body in disease as in health must be in harmony with the laws of life, true to the highest interests of the body and therefore RIGHT, it does not seek to suppress or control symptoms.

Dr. Jennings replied to a physician who had asked him in what respects he (Jennings) differed from many physicians of that day who employed but few drugs in these words.—*Medical Reform*, p. 306.

"We differ in two fundamental particulars:—

"*First*, the general principles on which we form our indications of treatment are directly opposite to each other. You hold that disease is wrong action; I maintain that it is right action.

"*Second*, to be consistent, the general rule for practices based upon your general principle must be break up diseased action. On my general principle, let diseased action alone."

Again:—

" 'That is all very well,' said a good friend, 'in mild disease, but when disease becomes violent, if there is nothing done to check it, it will overcome the powers of life.' This friend admitted that disease was not a some thing, emphasizing the word thing. It must be a *some*-thing or a *no*-thing; and Orthopathists are content to let *nothing* take care of itself. But just here is the tug of war; the pivot on which the question of medicine or on medicine hinges. Admitting that mild diseases do not of themselves afford a basis for a system of medication, the question arises, 'does the extension or aggravation of symptoms change the *nature* of disease?' "—*Tree of Life.* p. 187-8.

Let there be no overlooking of the main point—THE ESSENTIAL NATURE OF DISEASE. Is the tendency of vitality—for there is no other agency concerned—in the aggregate of movements called disease, right or wrong? This is fundamental Either ORTHOPATHY is right, or else, HETEROPATHY is right.

If the *right action* theory is correct, then the let-alone plan is right and the name attached to the group of symptoms present is of no consequence. The let-alone plan may be adopted from the outset. There need be no waiting for developments, no anxiety, lest we are treating for typhoid fever and the patient is developing menengitis. We may safely carry out the following advise of Jennings:—

"Don't stop to inquire what disease is about to be developed, whether pneumonia or measles. In Old School times—and I suppose those times are not quite 'already past'—physicians were sometimes puzzled to distinguish between these diseases, for often in their incipiency they are easily confounded, and when they were bleeding, blistering, and dosing to break up and keep back a pneumonia, and at length discovered it was a case of measles, they would immediately desist from their break-up efforts, and let the measles come out and develop themselves. Orthopathy has, no trouble or perplexity of this kind. ALL DISEASES ARE 'SELF-LIMITED' AND MAY BE PERMITTED TO MAKE A FULL DISPLAY OF THEMSELVES. WHETHER THE SYMPTOMS RUN HIGH OR LOW, LET THEM RUN TILL THEY HAVE HAD THEIR RUN OUT. 'THE HARDER THE BATTLE, THE SOONER OVER' AND THE LESS IT IS INTERFERED WITH, THE LESS THERE WILL BE OF IT, AND THE MORE LIKELY IT WILL BE TO END WELL. There can be no wrong action, for whatever action there is, is controlled by an immutable righteous law, which insures its tendency toward recovery, whether it reaches that point or not."—*The Tree of Life*, p. 186. (Cap. Mine).

Under this plan of treatment, too, there need be no waiting for developments, as it can be instituted from the very beginning of any case. The physician is called to see a patient presenting symptoms like these: rapid pulse, high temperature, loss of appetite, prostration, etc. What is the disease? It may be the beginning of pneumonia, typhoid fever, measles, spinal menengitis or any other acute febrile condition. He must await developments. The symptoms are not far enough advanced to enable him to make a differential diagnosis. His theory and practice calls for a specific treatment for each separate symptom complex. But he can't tell what the symptom complex is going to be. He can only give "expectant" treatment and await developments. Under Nature Cure treatment, this is not necessary. It is not even necessary for the disease to ever reach a stage where a special name can be given it. While the Allopath or Homeopath waits for such developments, the Orthopath is doing his best work.

Acute diseases are self-limiting. Their tendency is towards recovery and the patient will recover without treatment. In fact they are always better off without treatment than when they are subjected to the meddlesome interferenc that is usually given and which passes under the name of therapeutics.

In treating an acute disease, the first rule to learn is: DON'T DO IT. The disease, it must be remembered, is a vital process in self-defense. It is not to be treated, but permitted to run its natural course.

An acute disease is a more or less violent reaction against disease influence. It is usually sudden in its onset and does not last long. Pain and increased temperature are usually present, with a loss of appetite, a sense of weakness or exhaustion, etc. Except in mild cases, the person so affected is forced to go to bed and cease all other activities. This is a wise provision of nature to conserve energy. It is not to be supposed that the sick person has any less vitality or nerve energy when the acute symptoms set in than he had ten minutes or a half hour previous when he may have been ploughing, cutting wood, digging ditches or some similar work that requires strength and energy. But there is every reason to think that the energy that is used under ordinary conditions for the performance of such work has been withdrawn from these channels and is now being used in the effort to throw off the Pathoferic matter. Were this not true how could an organism already greatly enervated marshal enough energy to accomplish the extra work it is undertaking in acute disease?

If the work of house cleaning is to be successful, it is essential that the undivided attention of the organism be devoted to the curing process. For this reason, all activities that can be dispensed with temporarily and that have no direct bearing on the task of purification are stopped. The digestive process is temporarily suspended, little or no digestive juices are secreted, the appetite is cut off, the patient is forced to rest.

This brings us, then, to our first rule of practice in acute disease: The primary requirement is rest: Physical rest. Mental rest. Physiological rest.

PHYSICAL REST—is secured by putting the patient to bed and making him comfortable A comfortable bed should be arranged and kept clean. All bedding should be as *hard*, and all bed-clothing should be as *light*, as a due regard for comfort will allow. Soft beds that permit the patient to sink down into them are exceedingly debilitating and uncomfortable. Heavy covers weigh down upon the sick person and make him uncomfortable. They prevent rest. And, as Jennings truly declares, "in passing through a grave renovating process, rest, rest, REST, is the remedy."

No organ, however small and comparatively insignificant, is ever permitted to utter a note of protest or complaint until all the resources of power are low and the present stock of power consistently available to that organ is nearly exhausted. If an essential organ has been impaired or injured by any means whatsoever, it is proportionately the more important that early and careful heed be given to the saving of power at the first evidence of impairment, and it is especially urgent that the body should be carefully guarded against further injury in any and all of its parts, until its present damaged condition is thoroughly repaired and recovered from.

Where much, and perhaps everything, depends on the economical and undisturbed expenditure of a few feeble vital forces, no disturbing causes should be admitted and as the orthopathic care of the sick is founded on the fact that the tendency of the movements of life, in disease, all and singular, is to save life as far as this may be threatened; and especially to avert threatened danger to any of its organs, the first object to be aimed at in the conduct of any case is to shut down all unnecessary wastes-gates, that is, to place the body as far as this may be possible, under those conditions in which there shall be no unnecessary expenditure of its powers, in order that the organs that are called upon to accomplish the essential work of cure, but may otherwise be deficient in power, may receive added force.

THE HYGIENE OF ACUTE DISEASE

Give the *Law of Distribution* full scope in apportioning power to the various organs, and dispensing the powers of life as necessity demands. Let it withhold power from one organ or set of organs, and appropriate it to others, as the ultimate and highest good of the whole organism may require.

The first death to occur in the author's practice was that of a man, nearing sixty years of age, who had pneumonia. There had been a rapid decline of symptoms. At the end of five days there were no fever, pains in chest, coughing, or other acute symptoms. I instructed him to remain in bed and remain perfectly quiet until one week later, when I would call again. Instead of following my instructions, he felt so good that he got up on the second day and sat up for over an hour. He talked much and tired himself greatly. Upon walking to his bed to lie down again, he "felt something break and fall" in his lungs. In a few hours thereafter he was in a coma from which he revived for a few hours, after it had lasted twenty-four hours, then lapsed back into the coma and in another twenty-four hours was dead. I am certain that had he remained quietly in bed, as instructed, until his lungs had fully repaired themselves and resolution was complete, he would be alive to this day. But he had been misled by reading the fallacious and often fatal advice to be up and around when you feel like it, because to remain in bed is to "give up to disease," and to be active stimulates the vital processes.

When it becomes plainly evident that the vital forces are to be severely tasked and tested in a curative, renovating, and defensive process, there should be no unnecessary delay in placing the body and mind under conditions and circumstances in which the forces of life can carry forward their work with the least possible interruption or loss of power. The mind should be set at ease, the body made comfortable, the conditions of recovery supplied, and no means employed to control the operations of the body or the symptoms of the renovating process. As fast as the *Law of Limitation* is enforced, and activity becomes tedious or wearisome, the body should be yielded up, and not the slightest obstacle placed in the way of the operation of any of the laws and forces of the vital economy. No fallacious theories about food or exercise adding to your powers and helping you "throw off" the disease should be permitted to cause you to continue active and to continue eating. Mental, physical and physiological rest are needed and the quicker these are secured, the more rapidly will be your recovery, and the less will be your suffering.

The evidences of a developing disease are indications that vitality is low, and its expenditure should be cautiously guarded. Nature never permits a single fiber of the body to deviate in its action from the normal state, or to suffer pain, so long as she can prevent it consistently with the general welfare of the body. Where there is much or continued complaining by parts of the body every waste-gate should be closed in order to conserve power.

If appetite and the desire to be about continue, it is permissible to eat lightly and to be lightly active, however, a quicker recovery will be made and a more comfortable sickness will be experienced if one ceases even these. "Keep still," says Dr. Jennings, "Rest, rest, REST, is the grand panacea."

If your body is in a disabled condition, and you are about to undergo a renovating process, or if it is already in operation, avoid exposure to all sources of additional damage to the body, at least until you are restored to a healthy condition. Exposure to cold, extreme heat, fatigue, excitement, grief, shock, physical violence or injury, etc., all lessen the chances of recovery. Many of the fatal cases of disease that are daily reported, are rendered so by the additional burdens imposed upon the powers of life, which a little prudent foresight might easily have prevented.

In many cases, the vital operations are kept so incessantly harassed by drugs, serums, operations, and treatments of various kinds, that they are kept so busy defending the body against these, they are not able to repair the original damage, or eliminate the cause of the original trouble.

Nothing should be permitted to interfere with a full and free operation of the laws of life, and the full development of disease. How extensive these developments may need to be we have no means of knowing, accurately, until the process is completed. Therefore, the appropriation and distribution of the vital forces that may be made in the particular circumstances, should be freely submitted too. "If this carries a man," says Jennings, "into a pleurisy, let him have a pleurisy; if it brings on typhus fever, bilious fever, or yellow fever, let him have that fever; if it plunges him into a deep lung affection, threatening confirmed consumption, let it have free course and push him as far in that direction as it will, for safety lies only in that direction; if it throws him into a fit, let him remain in the fit, until he is released from it 'by law.' Remember the words of Napoleon. 'We are a machine made to live. We are organized for that purpose; such is our nature. *Do not counteract the living principle. Let it alone; leave it the liberty of defending itself—it will do better than your drugs*'." —*Medical Reform*, p. 326-27.

Bodily warmth is essential to physical comfort and rest. If the sick person becomes chilled, and unless in high fever, he chills easier than a normal person, he is made uncomfortable, and elimination is checked. "Keep the feet warm is a prescription of universal application," said Dr. Walter. "By keeping the feet warm, the whole surface is correspondingly warmed, and the circle of circulation enlarged, and the labor of the heart correspondingly reduced."

Whatever its saving to the heart, if the body is kept warm, its energies are conserved and the processes of elimination are not interfered with. By keeping warm, however, is not meant to roast in an electric cabinet, or stew and boil in a hot bath. A comfortable warmth of the body maintained by a moderate amount of clothing and supplemented by a hot water bottle, or a jug of hot water, or an electric pad to the feet, is sufficient.

The patient should be made comfortable at all times. All his needs should be attended to carefully and gently. He should not be pampered or petted. Petting and pampering patients builds the sick habit. It produces self-pity and causes the patient to magnify his troubles. Firmness is essential, while care should be confined to the essentials.

MENTAL REST—It is of first importance that the mind be at rest. The sick man or woman should have perfect confidence in the power of nature to accomplish the work begun. The alarm and anxious concern of relatives, friends, and neighbors, must be met as resolutely as possible. It would be well if every individual could give the whole subject of disease a careful and thorough examination while he or she is yet well, and make up the mind then what course shall be pursued when ill. Sickness is not the time to examine the merits of the clashing and conflicting theories and practices now in vogue. Strive to get and habitually maintain a correct idea of disease so that when you become sick, if you are foolish enough to do so, your mind may be allowed to rest at ease in the perfect confidence that all that can be done to good purpose will be done by due course of law.

Where this has not been done those who have the care of the sick in their hands should take heed of every word, act or appearance, that may tend to shake the confidence of the sick person. Anxious faces, forlorn looks, and manifest fear are quickly discerned by the sick person and these weigh heavily upon him or her. Try to be cheerful and optimistic in the sick room. Your own confidence will help to buoy up the confidence of the sick person.

Mental rest is best secured by assuring the patient that he is in no danger and removing from his environment any mentally distractive object or sound. Especially should visitors be excluded from the room. The sick room is too often a visiting rendezvous where friends and relations congregate and talk. They recite all the ugly details of how Mr. or Mrs. so-and-so had this or that disease, how he or she suffered, how long he remained sick and how he or she died. Such talk is not calculated to create a peaceful, restful state of mind in the patient. Besides, the noise itself is distracting to a sick man. The habit of the "mental healer" of spending from a half hour to hours at the bedside of a patient chattering to him a lot of mummery which he neither understands nor appreciates, should never be permitted. It tires the patient and leaves him much weakened.

In his *Hygienic Handbook*, Trall roundly condemned the habit of making the sick room a visiting rendezvous where friends, neighbors and relatives congregate and talk, often, far into the night. In his *Water-Cure for the Million*, (p. 31-2), he says:—

"The usual custom and manner of watching with the sick is very reprehensible. If any persons in the world need quiet and undisturbed repose, it is those who are laboring under fevers and other acute disease. But with a light burning in the room, and one or more persons sitting by, and reading, talking, or whispering, this is impossible. The room should be darkened, and the attendant should quietly sit or lie in the same or in an adjoining room, so as to be within call if anything is wanted. In an extreme case, the attendant can frequently step lightly to the bedside, to see if the patient is doing well; but all noise, and all light should be excluded, except on emergencies. It is a common practice with watchers to awaken the patient whenever he inclines to sleep *too soundly*. But this is unnecessary, because when the respiration becomes laborous, the patient will awaken, spontaneously. Under the drug-medical dispensation, the custom is to stuff the patient, night and day, with victuals, drink or medicines, every hour or oftener, so that any considerable repose is out of the question. But, fortunately for mankind, the Hygienic system regards sleep as more valuable than the whole of them."

Stuffing the patient with food, drink and medicine, at all hours or half-hours of the day and night, not only disturbs rest and sleep by frequently awakening them to take these things, but these things keep the system in a state of excitement, add to the discomfort and suffering of the sick person, and make rest and sleep almost impossible. Most of the sufferings of the acutely sick, are due to the treatment and care they receive.

Brilliant light disturbs rest. The sick room should be both light and airy but not brilliantly lighted. The habit of keeping a light burning all night in the sick room is a bad practice and one to be avoided. It is sun-light alone that is of value to the sick. They should not be denied this, but at night, the dark room is conducive to sleep. The blinds need not be drawn during the day. I have always insisted that the sun-light be permitted free access to the sick room. Even in measles, where light is commonly regarded as very injurious to the eyes; I have insisted on open windows and raised shades and I have yet to see a single case in which any damage was done to the eyes. Indeed, I am convinced that the opposite and prevailing course will, and frequently does, injure the eyes.

Sleep is the highest form of rest. During sleep, all the reparative and recuperative processes go on most efficiently. The sick should be permitted to sleep as much as possible and should not be awakened for any reason whatsoever, except, of course, where cleanliness demands it. But sleep should not be confounded with the stupor that follows the use of narcotic drugs.

Noise disturbs rest and sleep. It is irritating to the sick person, much more so than to the well. All noise should be eliminated as far as possible and the sick person should make every effort to relax his or her mind, acquire poise, and be disturbed as little as possible by the remaining noise. Absolute quiet is essential in low stages of disease. Even the little noise caused by walking across the floor is irritating and should be avoided as much as possible. No one should be allowed in the room save the nurse, and no talking to the patient should be permitted.

PHYSIOLOGICAL REST—Is secured partly by the two preceeding rests—physical and mental rest—and by stopping the food intake. A certain amount of functional activity is essential to the continuance of life. Suspended animation is, no doubt, a fact in Nature, but it cannot continue for very long without ending in death. Aside from this essential activity, the activity of our physiological economy is largely determined by our food intake. To stop the food intake takes a heavy load off the internal economy. The work of digesting and assimilating food and of discarding the waste and refuse portions all ceases. The heart and lungs have less work to perform. The liver and kidneys are given a rest. In fact, the whole physiology is given a rest. The energy usually employed in digesting and assimilating food is now used for eliminating or neutralizing the toxic matter that is forcing the reaction.

There is no danger of starving to death. The human body can go for weeks and months with only water and air. Food that is eaten in acute disease does not nourish anyway. The more the patient eats, the worse he becomes so that the danger lies really on the other side.

All food should be withheld from the patient who is suffering from an acute disease until all acute symptoms subside. As long as there is any pain, fever of inflammation or other troubles, to give food is to add to the trouble. This is, then, rule two: IN ALL ACUTE DISEASE, DON'T FEED.

All the water may be allowed that the patient desires. There is no need, however, of forcing the patient to drink large quantities of water on the absurd theory that it increases the elimination of poisons.

The following quotation from Trall is to the point in this connection:—

"Food should not be taken at all until the violence of the fever is materially abated, and then very small quantities of the simpliest food only should be permitted, as gruel, with a little toasted bread or cracker, boiled rice, mealy potatoes, baked apples, etc. There is not a more mischievous or more irrational error abroad in relation to the treatment of fever than the almost universal practice of stuffing the patient continually with stimulating animal slops, under the name of 'mild nourishing diet,' beef tea, mutton broth, chicken soup, panada, etc. The fever will always starve out before the patient is injured by abstinence, at least under hydropathic treatment, and the appetite will always return when the system is capable of assimilating food."—*Hydropathic Encyclopedia*, vol. 2, p. 84.

In speaking of the treatment of smallpox, Dr. Shew declared, *Hydropathic Family Physician*, p. 429:—

"Most fever-patients are allowed to eat too much. Some may be allowed too little; but this must be the exception to the rule. In all severe fevers, the system absolutely refuses all nourishment; that is, it is not digested or made into blood. Hence all nutriment, in such cases, is worse than useless, since if it does not go to nourish the system, it must only prove a source of irritation and harm. If the disease is severe, then it would be best as long as the fever lasts, to give no nourishment whatever. In mild cases it would of course be otherwise, although it would harm no one to fast a few days, but would, on the contrary, do them good. When nourishment is given, it should be of some bland and anti-feverish kind. Good and well-ripened fruit in its season would be especially useful, taken always at the time of a regular meal."

Dr. Jennings wrote:—

"The great, extensive, and complicated nutritive apparatus, that requires a large amount of force to convert raw material into a living structure, is put at rest, that the forces saved thereby may be transferred to the recuperative machinery within their respective limits, so that there is no call for food, and none should be offered until the crisis is passed, or a point reached where some nutritive labor can be performed, and there is a natural call for nutriment. ****And food has no more to do with the production of vitality, than the timber, planks, bolts and canvas for the ship have in supplying ship-carpenters and sailors. In the mass of diseases—such as simple, continued, or remittent fever, scarlet fever, measles, mild bilious fevers—and most of the disorders that are termed febrile, that require a few days to do up their recuperative work in the proper course of treatment to be pursued, is exceedingly plain and simple. So long as there is no call for nutriment, a cup of cool water is all that is needed for the inner man."—*Tree of Life*, p. 187-7.

Dr. Tilden sagely observes:—

"Given any one of these so-called diseases, from a cold to smallpox, and the only logical treatment is to stop food, wash out the bowels with enemas, and rest. A physic irritates, enervates and further checks elimination; to feed adds to the decomposition in the stomach and bowels. Such treatment builds disease; and if the patient is old or very young, the remaining resistance may be overcome by a continuation of the same treatment and death result. Nothing but rest, rest from everything, restores nerve energy and establishes secretion and elimination. Forcing remedies act the opposite. Every illness is an effort at house-cleaning, and all the aid that nature needs is to be left alone.

"This is hard to believe for a profession spooked on the idea of cure. Toxemia is the only disease. Enervation checks the elimination of toxin. At every opportunity vicarious elimination takes place. An indigestion creates irritation of the stomach, and elimination of toxin takes place through the mucous membrane of the stomach. This is called catarrh of the stomach. Cold air irritates a sensitized mucous membrane of the throat and nose, Catarrh follows. Every toxemic crisis is brought about in the same way. Rest cures; food and drugs add to the so-called disease."—*Philosophy of Health*. Aug. 1924.

Again he says:—

"Rest, with all that the word implies, cannot be preached too strongly. It does not mean to stay in bed and eat and take drugs. Food and drugs stimulate, which is opposed to rest. Mental poise is restful, and must go with physical rest. So strong is the ingrained belief in food, that there will be readers who will insist that patients in the state in which young Coolidge is should be in bed. (This was written while young Calvin Coolidge was ill and his spectacular physicians were making their spectacular efforts to save him. Author.) No; if feeding is all that is necessary, such invalidism would not evolve. Such patients are taxed to death by food. A limited amount of properly selected food at the right period of such lives, would forestall such catastrophes; but when profound enervation and Toxemia are once evolved, there is but one way out of the trouble—but one treatment—namely, a wise, scientific letting-alone. This must be started before an insignificant accident like a friction blister starts an infection conflagration. A half-extinguished match has fallen in the wrong place many times, as history has recorded."—*Philosophy of Health,* Aug. 1924.

AIR: A plentiful supply of oxygen is one of the prime necessities of life, at all times. Deprive a man of all oxygen and death results in a few minutes. The need of oxygen is more urgent in disease than at other times, except, of course, when under violent exertion. The sick person cannot breathe without air. The sick-room should be well ventilated both day and night with the purest air obtainable, coming directly from the outside, and not from an adjoining room or hall or from a foul courtyard.

WATER: All the water may be given that thirst demands. One may rely implicitly upon instinct in this regard. Those who doubt the competency of man's natural instincts often insist on copious water drinking, even in the absence of any natural demand for such. This practice is not only not necessary, but it is decidedly harmful. Water should be as pure as can be obtained and may be given warm or cool, as relished most by the patient.

CLEANLINESS: It is difficult to over-estimate the importance of cleanliness. Not merely the patient, but his clothing, bed, room, the air he breathes, and his surroundings should be kept clean.

Cellars, yards, cess-pools, out-houses, garbage cans, slop-jars, dead and decomposing animal and vegetable matters, pools of stagnant water, hog-pens, cow-pens, stables, near the house, are prolific sources of disease. An environment reeking with the emanations from these is not fit for well or sick.

The sick person should be gently sponged with warm water once daily, or more often, if cleanliness demands it. The eyes, nose, mouth, throat, anus, opening of the vagina under the prepuce, should all receive particular care. Plain warm water will do to cleanse these, but if the need for something else is felt, dilute lemon juice is preferable to soap or antiseptics. This may be used as an eye wash, a mouth wash, or as a gargle for the throat, and for cleansing the surface of open sores.

In diphtheria, the patient should be placed face down, with the head a little lower than the body, to cause the throat to drain outward and the excretions to be spit out:—

Dr. Tilden says:—

"In pseudomembranous inflammation, (diphtheria, membranous croup) of the throat, everything should be done to avoid breaking or loosening up the membrane; for the more it is interrupted, the greater the local poisoning, and the more toxins there will be swallowed to be neutralized by the stomachic secretions.

"Positively nothing is to be put into the child's mouth; not a drop of water, for swallowing must be avoided. The act of swallowing breaks the mebranous protection. The old treatment of gargling and swabbing, was barbarous and, for intelligent people, criminal.

"Thirst must be controlled by frequent small enemas of water. Nourishment is not life-saving, as many think, but positively disease and death-provoking.**** From the foregoing explanation, it is obvious how dangerous is the old-time practice of swabbing and gargling the throat. No wonder the mortality was great, and no wonder the anti-toxin treatment has proved such a success. Its success, however, has been of a negative character—on the order of the lesser evil. If the anti-toxin has any influence—if it is not inert—it certainly must make a change in the nervous system; and this change must be reconciled and an equilibrium or readjustment take place, before a normal healing process can be resumed.'—*Impaired Health*, vol. 1, 271.

In cases where there is infectious matter, as in erysipelas, etc., care should be exercised not to carry the infection to another part of the body.

THE BOWELS: The bowels are usually points of great concern to doctors, nurses, patients, relatives and friends. Pills, powders, enemas, suppositories, etc., are frequently resorted to, to force these to act. Indeed, it is no uncommon thing to see the bowel goaded with cathartics or flushed with water, even when it is already moving freely and frequently. So deeply ingrained is the belief that we must DO SOMETHING, anything, so long as something is done, the physician and patient and all concerned, are not satisfied unless the body is being excited and stimulated.

A sound, vigorous body, with pure sensibilities, neither needs nor courts any kind or degree of unnatural excitation, but disdains and resists it in toto; and an impaired body and sensibilities, needs it no more, disdains it no less, and is less able to bear its devastating effect. "Stimulants," says Jennings, "act on the principle of the spur, 'increase action, but diminish the power of that action,' *always* leave less of power in any part on which they expend their action than there was in that part before they acted upon it." (*Tree of Life*, p. 198.) Shall we, then, exhaust the power of the bowels, and consequently, of the whole system, by forced labor, or shall we allow them to rest and recuperate?

Says Dr. Tilden:—

"There is a continual tendency in the minds of those who give thought to medical subjects (professional and lay) to think of bowel evacuation and elimination as identical. Consequently, when enervation has brought elimination to almost nil, doctors and patients use eliminating remedies. (?); and when the bowels are forced to move, the bladder to empty, the skin to act, etc., etc., they think elimination has been established. Not so—only voiding what has already been excreted. This is an old medical error of confusing excretion or elimination with evacuation or voiding, and much suffering and many deaths have been caused by the practice of forcing the bowels to move. Irritating drugs act in the opposite way from what is desired. They may force voiding, but always check excretion or elimination, and build Toxemia."—*Philosophy of Health*, Aug. 1924.

Dr. Page observed:—

"Tanner had no movement during his fast; Griscomb's experience was similar, and Connolly, the consumptive, who fasted for forty-three days, had no movement for three weeks, and then the temporary looseness was occasioned by profuse water-drinking, which in his case, proved curative."—*The Natural Cure*, p. 112.

Dr. Tilden records the case of a man suffering with appendicitis or something else, whose bowels moved on the nineteenth day. They moved twice that day—two very large movements of fecal matter, pus and blood, with a "dreadfully offensive" odor. Dr. Tilden gives it as his experience that in such cases it "usually requires from fourteen to twenty-eight days" for the bowels to move.

In discussing a case of typhus fever, which he cared for and in which there was no bowel action for a period of three weeks, Jennings says:—

"The special object in noticing this case, is to call attention to one feature of the disease, to wit: the suspension of the peristaltic, or natural downward motion of the bowel, for the long period of three weeks.**** Some of the friends of Mr. G. felt a concern for the quiet state of the bowels, and for *this concern*, I prescribed some pills which I knew 'would do no hurt, if they did no good.' For myself, I had no fear about the bowels, and should have had none if they had been kept at rest three weeks longer, if there had been no other sign of danger."—*Philosophy of Human Life*, p. 176-7.

I know of no more reason for forcing bowel action than for forcing heart action or lung action. Bowel action is automatic, and, except in cases of obstruction, may be confidently expected to do all the work that is really essential and to conserve all the energy possible by failure to act, when there is no urgent necessity for them to act. Even in obstruction, they usually succeed in sending the feces back the way it came and get rid of it.

Purgatives, laxatives and enemas, are sources of excruciating pain in cases of appendicitis, inflammation of the colon, etc., and are frequent causes of a break in nature's defense, resulting in a rupture of the bowel wall or a rupture of the appendix into the abdominal cavity instead of into the colon.

"Doctor," once said an anxious captain to Dr. Jennings, "my wife can't breathe much longer unless you do something for her." "Captain," replied the doctor, "Your wife can't stop breathing if she tries." Then he proceeded to administer some colored water and some "powders" composed of corn starch. After a short time, the lady's difficulty in breathing was relieved and she recovered, thanks to the potent "medicines" which she had received.

A fact, unknown, to physicians and laymen alike, is that all the functions of the body are performed with as much promptness, regularity, and efficiency as, under existing circumstances, is compatible with the safety and highest welfare of the body. In "disease" and in "health," that is, so long as life lasts, every organ and tissue of the body is at its post, ready and disposed to perform its particular functions, to the full extent of its abilities. They do good work when they have the power to do so, and when lacking in power to produce a perfect work, must do the best they can.

There are many ways of forcing increased action in debilitated organs for a brief period, providing there is enough power in reserve to produce the action, but these things always and necessarily, diminish the power of that action and do so in precisely the degree to which they accelerate the action. The increase of action is occasioned by the extra expenditure of power called out, not supplied, by the compulsory process, and therefore the quantity of power is diminished by this amount. The power is wanted for other purposes and will be used more judiciously and advantageously by the undisturbed law of appropriation, and distribution of the living system.

These facts apply equally to the bowel as to the heart or lungs or liver. We may depend on the body to regulate its own internal conduct to its own best interests.

PAIN: The relief of pain is an unmitigated evil. Most of the work of physicians consists in relieving pain and discomfort and almost invariably they "relieve" these with agents and by means that themselves produce more pain and discomfort than they "relieve." So true is it, that all drugs produce, as their *secondary* effects, the exact opposite to their *primary* effects, that Dr. Jennings suggested that drugs should be classified according to their *secondary* effects. Tonics should be called *debilitators*, pain-killers should be pain-producers, etc.

Pain is merely a symptom. Symptoms are such only and not cause. The office of pain is beneficial, protective. It may serve as a diagnostic guide, if it is not suppressed. Its suppression does not remove cause, but does retard or actually prevent recovery. "Grin and bear it," is the best advice ever given a patient in relation to pain or discomfort.

FEVER: Nothing better than a high fever can come to the sick person. The higher the fever, the quicker the recovery. No effort should be made to suppress, reduce or control fever. There is no reason to fear fever. The idea that two, three, four or more degrees of fever destroys the tissues of the body is arrant nonsense. A temperature of a hundred and four or a hundred and six certainly is not the fierce burning process some would have us believe it to be.

"Let the *manner* of its (animal heat) production be what it may. ****it must be under the control of vitality, ****it never rises more than seven, eight, or nine degrees above the healthy standard**** this may be uncomfortable, but can do no serious mischief. ****There is no wrong action."—*Medical Reform*, p. 132-3-4.

DELIRIUM AND CONVULSIONS: These are symptoms, *right actions*, and should not be suppressed. Their causes or occasions may kill, but these never do. So long as the occasion for these is present, they should be present. Their suppression by depressing the nervous system is injurious in the extreme.

COLLAPSE: This is a frequent phenomenon under the *sustaining* plan of treatment. It is an exceedingly rare thing under orthopathic care and is confined almost exclusively to old people. Collapse, under the methods in vogue, usually means death. This is so because the method of treating collapse is simply an increase of the methods that have produced it. If these methods are abandoned, recoveries are frequent.

If relatives, friends, nurses and physicians, upon whom the responsibilities for care of the case rest, can exercise the needed patience and not become panicky, recovery is reasonably certain in most cases. If the air of the room is kept pure, the temperature of the patient warm and equable, absolute quiet maintained, and the patient left alone, with only a little water touched to the lips and mouth at intervals, and some permitted to be swallowed when there is power of deglutition, resuscitation will occur.

However, if the usual mad-cap endeavors to save life are resorted to, if heart stimulants, respiratory stimulants, and various other perturbating measures are employed, there will be a sudden flaring up of the powers of life, as though the patient is improving and these powers will be exhausted in this final flare, and death will end the scene.

Dr. Jennings once suffered with a case of acute pleurisy. He has left us the following observations of his experiences, during this illness, which observations Dr. Oswald declared "deserve to be framed in every hygienic sanitarium." I desire to introduce these at this place.

"In January, 1840, the eighth month of my residence in a Western state, my general health began to decline. My appetite and strength gradually failed me; exercise became irksome, attended with great lassitude and a sense of soreness over the whole system, which at length made my couch and a recumbent posture desirable. While sitting up one evening, in preparation for the night's repose, I had a chill and a heavy rigor pass over me, shaking my whole frame, and making my teeth chatter, which continued for two or three minutes. As the chill subsided, a pain commenced in the top of my left shoulder, soon became agonizing, and after some ten or twelve minutes, gradually descended by the shoulder blade until it became fixed and exceedingly distressing in my left side, and whence, like a dense cloud, it spread through all the middle region of the chest, and in a short period, I was in a confirmed, acute inflammatory pleurisy. For twelve hours breathing was at best laborious, and painful, confining me to nearly an erect position in bed; but the distress occasioned by efforts at coughing was indescribable.

"The confidence of my wife in the 'let-alone' treatment, which had been strengthening through a number of years, and had carried her unflinchingly through a number of serious indispositions, on this occasion, faltered, and she begged me to send for a physician to bleed me or do something to give at least temporary relief; for, said she, 'you *cannot* live so.' In my own mind there was not the least vestige of misgiving respecting the course pursed.

"In view of the constitutional defect in the pulmonary department of my system, and the nature and severity of the symptoms, it appeared to me very doubtful whether the powers of life would be able to accomplish what they had undertaken and put me again upon my feet. But I felt perfectly satisfied that whatever could be done to good purpose would be done, by 'due course of law.' ****My mind, therefore, was perfectly at ease in trusting Nature's work in Nature's hands. There was no danger in the symptoms, let them run as high as they would. They constituted no part of the real difficulty, but grew out of it. The general movement which made them necessary, was aiming directly at the removal of that difficulty. INSTEAD, THEREFORE, OF BEING TROUBLED WITH SUCH SYMPTOMS, MY CONVICTION WAS VERY STRONG THAT I COULD LIVE BETTER WITH THEM THAN WITHOUT THEM, (caps. mine, author).

"In the morning, ten or twelve hours from the beginning of the cold chill, there was some mitigation of suffering, which continued till afternoon, when there was a slight exacerbation of symptoms; but the heaviest part of the work was accomplished within the first twenty-four hours. From that time, there was a gradual declension of painful symptoms, till the fifth day, when debility and expectoration constituted the bulk of the disease.

"Full bleeding at the commencement of the disease, followed by the other 'break-up' means usually employed in such affections, would have given me immediate relief and, by continuing to ply active means (for there would have been no stopping of it, short of stopping the action of the heart), the strongest, most distressing, and critical part of the disease might have been pushed forward to the fifth day; and I might even then possibly have recovered. But, granting that my life would have been spared, I suffered much less on the whole, under the 'let-alone' treatment than I should have done under a perturbating one, besides having the curative process conducted with more regularity, made shorter, and done up more effectually."—*Medical Reform*, p. 312.

COMPLICATIONS: A little boy became sick. A doctor was called. He said appendicitis and advised an operation. The boy was taken to the hospital. At the hospital, he was said to be suffering with typhoid fever. He was given an injection of serum. His brother removed him from the hospital the same day he was admitted. The author was called. He advised fasting and rest. The boy's condition grew better. After five days, the first doctor called again. He said the boy had a "touch of typhoid" and could not recover without food and drugs. He left two prescriptions. The brother tore these into bits. At the hospital when the brother took the sick child, the doctor in charge tried to impress him with the seriousness of the boy's condition. The brother replied: "He will be serious if I leave him here for you to feed and drug."

The brother was right. Feeding and drugging convert simple acute diseases, that should be well in two or three days to a week, into serious difficulties that last for weeks or months, and end in death or chronic disease. Drugs and feeding build complications. The boy only had a "touch of typhoid" because he did not receive typical text-book treatment. It takes typical text-book treatment to convert a simple fever into a typical text-book case of typhoid fever.

No disease can present all the symptoms attributed to it in standard text-books of medicine unless treated as outlined in these same text-books. Doctors build most of the pathology they spend years in studying. Feeding and drugging are the greatest sources of suffering and death in disease. An acute disease should be a comfortable illness. And it would be if the patient was given warmth, quiet, rest, air and water, and all feeding and drugging omitted. Death except in old age, would be extremely rare, and the length of human life would go upward with a bound.

If these suggestions are followed faithfully, and no drugs or serums are given the patient will be out of bed in a few days. Cases of typhoid fever, pneumonia, etc., which usually run three to four weeks or even longer, need not last more than seven or eight days to two weeks, providing these suggestions are followed from the very onset of the disease: In fact, these diseases will never develop into typical cases under this plan.

CONVALESCENCE: Is a period in which care must be exercised if the patient is to fare well. The body has just emerged from a severe fight. It is weak from the expenditure of much energy. There has been more or less destruction of tissue. The patient is in no condition to return to normal activities until he has thoroughly recuperated from his illness. A premature return to duties may easily prove disastrous.

The destroyed tissues must be repaired. The used up nerve force or vital force, must be recuperated. This requires time, although it takes place under proper conditions fairly rapidly. It is possible to hasten or retard the recuperation and reparation.

Over exertion, a return to the old destructive habits, over-eating, exposure to extremes of temperature, etc., may not only hinder recovery, but may actually work injury. On the other hand, recuperation may be hastened somewhat by proper attention being given to rest, sleep, exercise, diet, one's air supply and sunshine.

Rest is essential to recuperation of vital force. This we have already learned. Now consider the condition of the convalescing patient. He has already greatly enervated, else he would not have been toxemic and would not have become sick. He has just gone through a hard trying struggle which has left him much weaker than before. Rest must be enforced now, in order to recuperate.

Sleep, we have already learned, is the highest form of rest. If the patient can sleep much, this will hasten the recuperation. He should lie down at intervals during the day and attempt to sleep. No sitting up until late hours at night should ever be permitted. He should retire early.

During the process of disease there was more or less destruction of tissue. This must all be repaired before the organism is ready to resume normal operations. This requires some time and necessitates rest. Tissue repair is only accomplished during rest and reaches its maximum point of efficiency during sleep. Thus we have an added reason for rest and sleep.

By the foregoing, is not meant that the patient should lie in bed or sit in an invalid's chair and rest and sleep twenty-four hours out of every day? On the contrary, we insist that a small amount of mild exercise be taken daily and that the amount taken be gradually increased.

Life and health demand a certain amount of exercise. Even plants must have exercise if they are to do well. Plants get their exercise in a passive form, that is, the wind as the operator, gives them passive exercise.

There are times when exercise would be highly injurious, but outside of these, a certain amount of exercise is essential to good health and strength. So in convalescense, the patient who exercises judiciously will recover faster than the one who does not. He must not attempt a hundred-yard dash or enter a weight-lifting contest by any means. His exercise should be moderate, and of short duration. He should not exercise until tired or exhausted. As he grows stronger, he can exercise more strenuously, and exercise longer.

Walking is the favorite form of exercise. For my part, I could never see why it should be better than other forms as long as they are not carried to excess. The safe rule is moderation. Take the exercise you derive most pleasure from.

Feeding in convalescence is a very important item. The digestive organs are still weak, their secretions are not normal so that they are by no means fitted to handle a "square" meal. Great care must be exercised in breaking the fast which the patient has been on.

If the disease has been of such a nature that there is likely to be any ulcerations or open sores in the intestinal tract time should be given for these to heal before food is given, and this applies especially to the feeding of solid foods. A small piece of solid food may easily become lodged in the ulcer, and produce irritation, set up fermentation, and cause infection.

Again, if food is given before the stomach, intestine, or bowel are thoroughly healed, the movements of these organs as they convey the food along, is likely to produce mechanical injury to the unhealed parts. A safe plan is not to be in too much of a hurry to feed.

To resume feeding, fruit juices or vegetables juices may be used. Here again should moderation be the watchword. Don't try to rush matters. *Nature does her work slowly, but well.*

After a day or two, small amounts of other foods may be added. The amount eaten should be gradually increased. Don't hurry.

Let the food be of simple wholesome nature. It should consist chiefly of fresh fruits and green vegetables. Starch foods, protein foods and fatty foods, should be used very sparingly. Some proteins are needed for repairs, but one does not have to eat these in large quantities.

Air and sunshine are as essential during convalescence as at other times. It would be well to spend as much time outdoors as possible. A hammock or chair under a tree makes an ideal resting place. Don't stay in the sun too much at first. Sleep with windows open so that fresh air can be yours at all times. The body needs plenty of oxygen in its work of reparation.

Don't allow yourself to become angry or excited. Don't indulge in card games or other such games that may excite and tire you. Keep out of exciting or distracting arguments. Keep away from exciting shows. Treat yourself decent and a quick return to normal will be yours. Your system will then be all the better for the house cleaning.

This is all very simple, so simple, indeed, that it doesn't seem possible that it will do the work. But if the reader has read and understood the foregoing chapters, he will readily understand how it is possible. In fact, he can easily see that this is the only logical way of treating the patient.

HYGIENE OF CHRONIC DISEASE

Chapter XXX

THE seomewhat unique principle is maintained by *Orthopathy*, that the first condition of successful restoration of health is a philosophical comprehension, by the sick person, of the cause or causes of the malady. All cure is self-cure and every sick person must cure himself or herself. The sick person must learn to distinguish between effects and their antecedents in order that he may not waste time, and perhaps irreparably injure his health, trying to remove or suppress effects by measures that do not correct or remove their antecedents. Dr. G. H. Taylor has so admirably expressed these facts in his *Pelvic and Hernial Therapeutics*, (1885) that we shall reproduce what he says.

"Morbid phenomena, especially those usually designated chronic disease, are regarded in one of two general ways. As these modes of estimating often lead to differing, even to opposing remedies for what is essentially the same morbid condition, it becomes important that the proper distinctions between these modes should be made.

"One way of estimating disease is that adopted by the patient and by sympathizing friends, and doubtless influences the physician to a large extent. This estimate is based upon subjective facts—what the patient feels, sees, and experiences. It includes his consciousness of defect of power and excess of sensibility, and the accompanying exterior manifestations.

"Remedies are therefore sought in accordance with these conceptions, and include prominently whatever means may be capable of mitigating, or even abolishing, disagreeable sensations, or at least the consciousness thereof, often with little reference to the source from which those feelings spring.

"The invalid, unfortunately for his own true interests, is disinclined to discriminate between the two distinct ideas of suffering and of disease. He blends the two as one. This leads to the radical mistake of trying to cure the one by causing suspension of the other. He seems to think that pain is causing him injury, instead of referring it to the morbid action from which the pain is derived. It is not the pain, —which is doubtless on the whole advantageous,—but its causes, which demands correction.

"It is therefore with difficulty that the invalid learns that while this and other subjective manifestations are undoubted verities, they alone are untrustworthy indications as to remedies because incomplete indications of disease. The facts of pathology are far more extended, and all, not a part, are required as a basis for any proper remedial prescription. Too close reliance on sensory indications inevitably leads to therapeutic difficulties. These consist in the mistakes of trying to remedy mere effects in place of removing their causes.

"Another consequence of undue regard to the subjective indications of disease, is the premature arrest of diagnostic inquiry. Further investigation, as the tracing of effects to their causes, is discouraged; the idea of philosophical relationships of seen and unseen facts is repressed, and the advantages to therapeutics of such inquiries become unavailable. The physician is guided by only a limited number of subordinate facts, which, being isolated from their true connection, are untrustworthy.

"A still further difficulty, usually indirectly expressed arising from the above stated sources of misconception, is the tendency in the popular mind to associate, in idea, defects of the vital organism with those of non-vital objects. Diseased manifestations are thought to be like something broken, requiring local repair by trained and dextrous hands. The remedy must accord with the immediate, patent, and obtrusive difficulty, as a broken implement is mended. Medical science is limited to the record of experience in correcting local faults of the organism and insufficiently correlates with science in its wider aspect.

"The defects of this mode of regarding chronic disease, and the practical therapeutic errors to which it inevitably leads, will be shown in succeeding chapters in connection with such affections as those pertaining to the pelvis and adjacent parts. These errors are so surprising, and so easily detectable that it is a wonder that the medical profession, trained to great acuteness in pathological observation, should not have long ago insisted on their correction.

"The other mode of estimating chronic disease in reference to remedies, regards its ordinary manifestatoins as only symptoms, products, and evidences of antecedent causes, without which such manifestations would be impossible. It therefore assumes that however distant and obscure these causes, they are the primary objects of medical interest, and of remedial attention. The actual departure from health is a *process* rather than a *product*. The objective phenomena are a cumulative record of transitional defects and errors. The physician points out and corrects these, and the consequences, however manifested, cease perforce. Nothing exists, not even local disease, after the withdrawal or cessation of the processes whereby it exists.

"This is the physiological method. This method regards health and disease as flowing from essentially identical sources, the difference consisting solely in the degrees of perfection attained by the inchoate activities at the ultimate sources of vital power. Remedies are therefore concerned in the control of precesses, rather than in obscuring the effects and products of these processes. The processes of physiology embrace the whole career of matter entering the organism, onward to its final exit. During this transit it is subjected to a series of changes, and a variety of differentiations in physical quality and form, for the sole ultimate purpose of evolving force or energy. The processes of physiology are minute, involving not merely the tissues of every part, but the ultimate molecules, and constituent elements, beyond the powers of ordinary observation; these may, but often do not, make an impression on the consciousness or sensibilities

"In the diseased state (indicated in medical science by the word pathology) there is the same career of the same matter, but under conditions less favorable for the attainment of perfected results. The changes due have in some stage of the career been imperfectly attained. In some local part, or by some inferior physical change, the progressing matters have failed to yield energy and *therefore*, and coincidently, failed to attain the chemical form necessary for exit. The product, both of energy and of substance, depends on processes in the respective organic instruments devoted to these purposes. Pathology, therefore has its potential existence in transitional acts, rather than in the form which the consequences of the imperfection of these acts assume. The distinction should always be made between the effects, consequences, and products of imperfect physiological processes, and the processes from which these evidences proceed. It is the former of which we are chiefly cognizant, because more exposed to observation; they are exterior and objective, and often present a cumulative mass. The latter are interior, elusive, and known by comparison and by the reasoning faculties.

"These considerations unmistakably imply a wide distinction between the inward, invisible and intangible form of disease, irrespective of the sensation, and the consequences thereof as exhibited in objective phenomena. The one is continuously contributing, by the changes occurring in successive particles of substance, to produce and maintain the other; the relation of cause and effect being precisely the same as that recognized as resulting in health. Pathology therefore exists less in formed product than in its forming. The impressions of consciousness may or may not exist, according to the nature and location of the imperfect process, and are always to be classed with the objective phenomena, or formed products, so far as relates to therapeutics. It is therefore a profound mistake to merge together as an undistinguishable whole two considerations so radically distinct as cause and effect, antecedent and consequent, process and product, in pathology; and such confusion of separate and different things inevitably introduces into practical therapeutics the gravest inconsistencies and mistakes.

"The adequate comprehension of disease therefore considers it in the two aspects above presented. These for convenience may be styled the antecedent and the resultant *factors*, meaning the defective processes, and the cumulative products.

"The susceptibility of the two distinct parts of pathological phenomena to separate consideration arises from the nature of vital processes, of which disease is but a form. These processes are progressive, and never concluded as long as life lasts. It probably extends throughout all the forms and variations of these processes, which receive distinct names, according to subordinate peculiarities. The evidence of this statement is derived from a variety of sources.

"Prophylactics, or the means of prevention of diseases, emphatically recognizes an antecedent principle and antecedent action. The malarial infections, zymotic and incubative affections generally, are confessed demonstrations of the same principle; and the same is legitimately inferred of acute affections having obscure sources though no less positive manifestations, but whose processes and products are so blended as regards time, that the distinction has less practical therapeutic value.

"The failure to recognize the distinction above pointed out as to antecedent and resultant parts or factors of diseases, opens the way for the perversion of therapeutics from its greater to its lesser uses. Remedies addressed to the resultant, or consequent object, are necessarily only palliative, and in general can have no effect on the contributive factors. The abatement of pain, one of the consequences of the morbid, or unperfected process, easily becomes the primary, instead of an incidental purpose. The sufferer is countenanced in his delusion that pain is something synonymous with disease, and that the latter disappears with it. Besides, a practical error of still more serious import is committed. The advantages of pain as a pathological guide are lost. Another and very disadvantageous consequence arises from medicating the sources of sensibility, which should not be the therapeutic purpose. These sensory powers are inevitably perverted by the constant use of remedies adapted to diminish pain, without paying attention to its causes. The nervous system is therefore liable ultimately to become an overwhelming factor, additional to the primary ones.

"The relations of the antecedents to the resultants in pathology are necessarily those of equality, because effects must proceed from adequate and therefore an equal cause; but this fact does not imply interchangeability, but the contrary. The latter always depends on the former, and not the former on the latter. Remove the morbid processes by converting them into healthful processes, that is, into perfected morphological and chemical activities, and the morbid effects, however conspicuous, cease to exist. No radical curative effect is attainable, if therapeutic attention be limited to the resultant factors; such medication may be palliative, but is devoid of direct control of antecedent processes. However deftly the consequences be removed nothing permanent is secured; the continuance of the producing factor is sure to reinstate the morbid result, however concealed, altered, or obscured to the senses.

"An intelligent appreciation of the distinctions above made, appears to be necessary to prevent medical practice from degenerating, as it is manifestly inclined, into a fruitless routine of palliative procedures. Methods of toying with the senses, and ways of disconnecting imperfect results from the elementary processes on which these results depend: devices in short for concealing these results mistakenly regarded as the disease, whether the manifestation be interior in the form of pain, or exterior in some outward tangible indication, as in the pelvis, or at the hernial border, assume unwarranted importance. The antecedents and the consequences, which are entirely distinct considerations become inextricably mingled in therapeutics and remedies adapted to radical cure, in the sense of correcting the primary departure from true physiological action, become impossible.

"One of the leading obstacles to the recognition, and therefore the remedying of the primary factors of disease instead of the resultant factors, cannot be too strongly insisted upon; one that imperils and often negatives the value of medical science. This practice is based on the presumption that the fact of pain is actually diminished by this class of so-called remedies. This is an assumption that is manifestly improbable; but, on the other hand there is much evidence showing that symptoms relating to the seat of consciousness may thus be easily deferred, and possibly their location changed, yet the amount of pain, taking time into consideration, is actually often very greatly increased by the method invoked to stifle it. These statements are necessarily confined in their application to chronic affections; for it is readily conceded that in acute affections nature is at work, repairing defects, and gaining ground by intensifying compensative processes, in spite of the temporary interference of medicaments when these have no relation whatever to reparation."

In overcoming any disease condition the problem is not so much one of overcoming the disease directly, as it is of attacking and overcoming the popular misconception regarding its essential nature. The mind of the patient and the minds of the patient's relatives and friends have first to be freed of the perverted views and erroneous theories of disease that have been and are being fostered by the medical profession.

The very expression "Cure" as used today is misleading and wrong. It is understood to require the expenditure of time, attention and energy on the part of the healer, attendants and patients upon a subject that should require no attention whatever. Disease should not exist at all and healing should be unnecessary. However, all real cure is self-cure and cannot be accomplished by outside agencies and skill.

The fact that millions of men and women are engaged in an effort to patch up the remainder of their fellow men and women is actually humiliating. In this particular we are lowered below the beasts of the fields and fowls of the air. In spite of all our boasted wisdom and science, in spite of our boasted superiority, we are not equal to the animals of the forest and plains in health and hardihood.

Man is capable of possessing a higher degree of health and vigor than any other animal on the face of the earth—yet he actually possesses far less than any other. Man alone requires, or THINKS HE REQUIRES to be in the shops for repairs. Man alone, except those animals he has enslaved, supports doctors, nurses, attendants and costly hospitals.

"Cure of Disease!" exclaimed Trall. "What a world of delusion in that expression! It has always been the fundamental error of the medical profession. It forever misleads the public mind. The phrase is founded on a false conception of the nature of disease. Instead of trying to cure diseases, we should seek to remove their causes. Diseases never can be and never should be cured while their causes exist. It is on the fallacy of curing disease that the doctors are drugging the world to death."
—*The Hygienic System.*

Some people possess an undying faith in the doctor and his methods. They possess more faith in the doctor than the religious man is supposed to have in his God. The doctor can do everything to them short of killing them and they trust him still. If there is any survival after death they probably retain their faith in the doctor and his methods even after these have killed him. Such faith is beyond all understanding; If faith had any curative power such patients should not long remain sick.

If they lose their faith in one doctor or in one system of "healing" it is only to transfer their allegiance to another doctor or to another system. They go from doctor to doctor, from institution to institution, from system to system but they never lose faith. They never get well because they never reform their lives. They are in search of cures and cures they will find if they have to die in the attempt.

About five years ago a prominent "Natural Therapist" triumphantly exclaimed:—
"My soul now rests in peace. My life-work is completed. I have witnessed the fulfilment of my heart's desire—the conquest of disease."

A year later this same man declared:—
"We are constantly testing new methods and we shall continue to incorporate in our system everything that gives positive results in the treatment of human ailments."

Today, five years after he made his first statement, the wonder-working machine that he had seen conquer disease is a thing of history. It has come and gone. Its heyday of popularity is over. Its day of miraculous accomplishment is passed. It has been "modified," and "improved" over and over again. Its inventor is dead. The man who made the above statement is dead. Other machines and apparatuses have come and gone. They enjoyed their day and followed it to oblivion.

"Natural Therapeutics," now obsolescent, was a Heteropathic system identical with Naturopathy. "Physiological Therapeutics" were of the same order. They each attempted to cure disease and each possessed many methods of "cure."

Dr. Walsh maintains in his "*Cures; The story of the Cures that Fail*," that in proper conditions of confidence literally anything will cure a large number of cases. This attributes the cure to the mental effects of the "remedy" and ignores, completely, the self-curative powers of the body. If his contention were true the more cases that were cured by some vaunted "cure" the greater would grow the confidence imposed in its curative virtues. The greater the confidence in the "cure" the more cures it would make and thus, the longer it was used the more effective it would become. A vicious circle would thus be established that would be self-perpetrating. A remedy, once popular would have little chance of ever losing its place in the confidence imposed in its powers. This is, however, contrary to what the history of the cures that failed (after they had literally "cured" their thousands and tens of thousands) reveal. Their period of popularity is usually brief. Dr. Walsh will have as much difficulty in trying to explain this fact in the light of his theory as he will in explaining how these same cures also "cured" infants, animals and plants. I do not believe the success of the "cures" in the cases of infants, animals, and plants can be explained with Dr. Walsh's assumption as a basis. It will either have to be admitted that the methods did possess some curative power at the time they were used, even if they did not possess it later, or else the self-curative powers of the organism will have to be recognized and given full credit. I do not deem it necessary that I here restate the Orthopathic position in the matter. I leave the matter up to the candid and thoughtful reader now, who, after having carefully weighted the evidence, should be able to decide whether or not our position is the correct one.

The effort to beat the laws of nature, to cheat cause out of its effect, by the use of remedies or medicines is so childishly absurd and so inherently impossible that man should long ago have realized his folly in persistently attempting such a thing. Any real and permanent cure (of an abnormal condition of the body) must be the result of a constitutional reconstruction within the body itself and this can only be brought about by the forces of nature that are concerned in growth, development, repair and maintenence of the animal and vegetable world. No form of artificial treatment (therapeutics) embodies these principles.

Every form of artificial treatment is sympotomatic and is in no wise directed at cause. To treat a patient merely symptomatically is most decidedly wrong. Symptoms are such only and not causes, and to direct attention to effects and ignore causes is like the effort to rid a swampy region of mosquitoes by swatting individual mosquitoes instead of draining the swamps. It is only patch work.

Dr. Walter has left us the following bit of wisdom, which, if rightly understood and heeded will free man from both ill-health and the cure mongers.

"Men try everything and fail to get well. Let them stop trying for a while and they will get better results. 'Not try but trust' is often as important to health as to religion. What most people want is more rest and less worry. Drowning men catch at straws but it is the catching at straws that drowns them. The drowning of people is almost invariably due to their struggles to save themselves. If they would lie quietly on the water, with nose elevated, they could float and breathe for hours; instead of which they plunge and roll and struggle, until, exhausted, they give up the contest and sink to rise no more. In the matter of health in our day, it were folly to be wise. Nearly all thought, all doctrine and all practice is opposed to good health. About all theories of disease are exactly wrong."—*Vital Science*, p. 177.

"Be still, and know that I am God." Be still. Cease to resist. Cease trying to overcome evil with evil. "Cease to do evil and learn to do good." "Be not overcome of evil, but overcome evil with good." "Go and sin no more." This is good Orthopathy as well as good religion. Man fights disease (which he conceives to be evil) with methods that are evil, while, at the same time, continuing the evils that are responsible for his disease. He has not and does not, "cease to do evil and learn to do good." The Orthopathic doctrine of Health by healthful living and cure by the same means, by learning to "go and sin no more," has never appealed to many. But it is as certain as anything that so long as he sows "to the flesh" he must continue to reap corruption.

Chronic diseases are usually considered to be incurable and we are sorry to have to say that they are usually not cured. Despite the noise that is made by many drugless institutions and by certain drugless practitioners about their wonderful success in dealing with chronic disease they do not accomplish as many wonders as their talk and writing would lead one to suppose.

This is equally as true of other systems of treatment. Chiropractors have in recent years been making a lot of noise about their wonderful cures of chronic diseases. Naprapaths, likewise, publish a list of wonders they have performed.

Now the truth about the whole matter is that these men never mention those cases in which they fail. And their failures are many. Again, many of their boasted cures are not cures at all. It often happens that a patient is pronounced cured, he writes an "unsolicited" testimonial at the request of the one who treated him, and in a week or a month is as bad as ever. These facts are not given to the public. When they talk, they tell of their successes or apparent successes, not of their failures. These things are all equally as true of those who "heal" by "mind power," "Divine power," etc.

The drugless professions are as much given to fads in treatment as the drugging professions. The whole human race indulges in fads, therefore the drugless "healers," being partly human, are afflicted with much of this human weakness. Only a few years back, hydrotherapy and mechanotherapy held the day. Water cure institutions filled our land. These were followed by osteopathy, this by such things as the vibrator, the beautfiul "violet ray," spondylotherapy. Then Chiropractic took the field. Chiropractic gave way to a conglomeration of all kinds of methods. These conglomerationists call themselves mixers and are usually mixed.

They have developed hosts of methods of treating ailments and invented myriads of instruments and appliances to do the work with. The office of a "mixer" reminds one of a store room or junk shop—sometimes we can see a resemblance in them of a Curio Shop. It seems that their inventive possibilities are never to be exhausted.

Medical men usually admit that they cannot cure chronic diseases, however sure they may be that they can cure the acute or self-limited forms. The drugless branches of Heteropathy, however, insist that they can cure chronic diseases. One psuedo-nature cure sanitarium that was formerly located in Chicago and which claimed to achieve remarkable results in the chronic forms of disease, used to give patients the following routine treatment each day. The patients were made to get out of bed at six o'clock in the morning. They then went into the basement where the treatment rooms were located and were given the cold blitz-gus, a high pressure stream of cold water, over their bodies, and particularly along the spinal column. From this they passed into the massage room where they received from twenty to thirty minutes of maulings and poundings and were shipped into another room for another twenty minutes of Sweedish movements. After this, an Osteopath played with the spine of each one for another ten minutes and they were sent up to dress for breakfast.. They were ready to go back to bed, of course, but instead of this, they were taken in the middle of the forenoon out of doors and given several minutes of exercise. In the evening, before retiring, each patient was given a cold sitz bath or a cold pack. Such treatment kept them in a state of vital depletion and "crises" were of frequent development.

The development of chronic disease has already been discussed considerably in previous chapters. We will content ourselves with but a brief recapitulation at this time.

Disease is vital action (in self-defense), abnormal because of abnormal conditions, and is occasioned by anything which is sufficiently disliked by the organism to war against it. If the organism is unable to overcome and destroy the condition or occasion for the fight, it is forced to either accommodate itself to the condition or perish.

The initial fight against any disease influence is an acute reaction (crisis) against it. If the acute effort fails to accomplish its purpose the organism attempts to accommodate itself to the condition and carry on the battle less vigorously and over a longer period of time. This gives us chronic disease.

Chronic disease, is therefore, usually the result of the same conditions that produce acute disease, with the added element of accommodation. The failure of the organism to overcome the disease influence by acute eliminative efforts is usually due to the suppressive methods used by the physician. Every abnormal symptom is suppressed as quickly as it arises. If, after one is suppressed, another appears, it is as quickly suppressed. This often results in the death of the patient. Here we cannot refrain from quoting the remark of Dr. Trall in reference to the death of General Taylor. He said: "When I heard of blackberries as among the causes of General Taylor's death, I thought of blue-pills, and gray powders, and green tinctures, and red lotions, and brown mixtures."—*True Healing Art.*

These same colored pills, powers, tinctures, lotions and mixtures are as effectively suppressing acute symptoms, and producing chronic disease or death today as they did in the days of Dr. Trall, only we have more of them and have serums, vaccines, anti-toxins, etc., to help them. The increase in Chronic disease keeps pace with our increasing means for suppressing acute forms.

The organism would, in most cases, be able to throw off the disease influence by the efforts it puts forth in chronic disease were it not that the condition that makes it necessary is kept alive by the prior habits. The chronic sufferer keeps up his enervating habits and weakening indulgencies. This, of course, perpetuates his condition and results ultimatly in more and greater trouble and varied forms of trouble. Every new phase in the development of chronic disease is prepared for by its precedents. The continuity of the process is nowhere broken. When a new stage "begins" which appears to be a new and distinct disease, or which presents a new and different form, it has been gradually prepared for beneath the surface of events. It is a serious blunder to single out each link in a series or chain of successive or concomitant developments and give to each of these a different name and ascribe them to different causes. They originate out of the same antecedents.

Elimination is accomplished by the body itself (if it is given an opportunity), but cannot be forced. But if the organs of elimination are given more work than they are able to perform the toxemia must continue to increase. If out-put does not equal income there is bound to be an accumulation of the residue within the system. If the patient is piling into his system by way of food, drink, tobacco, etc., more than the organs of elimination can send out, how is the patient to recover? If there is gastro-intestinal putrefaction resulting in the absorption of more toxic material than these organs can handle it must be stopped before recovery, can take place. Physiological rest will accomplish this.

As this process of toxin accumulation continues it reaches a point where life is endangered. The organism then institutes a crisis and eliminates it through other channels. Or perhaps there is exposure to cold or rain, or an unusual meal and a crisis is forced. These crises, however, do not result in health but succeed only in reducing the toxemia to the toleration point, after which the acute symptoms again subside. We then have a short period of what commonly passes for health during which there is more toxin accumulation followed by another crisis. This merry-go-round of toxin accumulation, followed by a crisis; then more toxin accumulation and another crisis keeps up until death puts a period to our existence.

Under hygienic conditions, as the body's powers are gradually raised the amount of toxic material it will tolerate is gradually lessened. As the body grows stronger, and the vital powers increase, the effort to become master increases. The organism often develops acute efforts to throw off the enslaving toxins. Thus we have the appearance of the healing crisis, in the recovery from chronic conditions. Often times, too, the body is able to eliminate the toxins without resorting to crises.

Chronic disease is a subdued effort at cure, resulting either from suppression of acute disease or from long continued indulgence in its causes. Chronic disease represents chronic provocation. It is kept alive from day to day, from year to year by continuance of the causes which have produced it.

The essential thing to remember is that there is an inherent tendency in the organism towards health and that a return to health will always follow the removal of the conditions and influences that are interfering with health, providing, of course, that some irreparable damage has not been done. Cure is accomplished by the forces and functions of the organism itself and not by so-called therapeutic methods. The office of the hygienist is to furnish the conditions that are required by the organism to enable it to accomplish its work of cure with the least amount of hindrance. Weakening and enervating influences can and should be removed. And these are the true methods of aiding Nature. Surgery is sometimes essential, especially in cases of accidents.

Orthopaths maintain that there are no incurable diseases, although there are incurable cases, which simply means that all cases are curable if causes are corrected in time, but all cases are incurable if allowed to advance too far. Degeneration may reach a point where regeneration is impossible, but until that point is reached any condition is curable. Curable by the body's own processes and functions. There are no therapeutic devices or agents, except in the sense that therapeutcis is the application of agencies for the suppression of symptoms. And it is just this more often than otherwise.

To show just what we mean by this let us take a look at the present practice of endocrinoloy. The facts and theories upon which the practice is based are contained in the following propositions:—

1 The endocrine glands secrete substances that are essential to normal metabolism and function.

2 Through some derangement of a gland, either functional or structural, the gland's secretion is either of poor quality, or is insufficient or excessive in amount, and produces certain functional and structural derangements in the body, depending upon the gland deranged and the nature of its derangement.

3 By means of various chemical, mechanical, or electrical agencies, or by food, etc., and by glandular extracts from animals the endocrine secertions may be modified or normalized. The action of the gland is either stimulated or inhibited.

The agent most commonly used for these purposes is powdered glands from animals.

The weak link in this chain lies in the fact that it does not go deep enough. It treats the deranged gland as though it were the primary cause. No attention is given to the reason for the glandular derangement.

The question is a pertinent one: Why are the glands deranged? Can the reason for their derangement be found and removed? The practice of stimulating or inhibiting the glandular derangement cannot give more than temporary relief.

As long as the cause or occasion for the glandular derangement is present the derangement will persist. If the interfering element be removed the gland will again become normal in its activities, providing it has not been irreparably damaged. And this is one reason we object to stimulating or inhibiting them, it hastens their destruction and at the same time leaves cause untouched, so that the glands reach a point where a return to normal is impossible. An intelligent practice will not allow degenerative changes to reach such a point.

Treatment of this nature may and often does produce temporary relief. However, no method or system of treatment can be properly judged by its immediate effect. A dose of opium, a cup of coffee, may produce an immediate feeling of well being, the eating of an orange may not produce such an effect. But if we look into the future and note the ultimate results we can easily decide which is the best. Our test must ever be the condition of the patient six months or a year after treatment.

Any method that attempts to overcome the effects of indulgence, uncleanliness, lack of self-control, sensuality, gluttony, inebriety, intemperance, etc., without correcting these can only end in failure. Nature has no plan of vicarious atonement. She demands obedience to her laws and exacts her penalties for every infraction of these.

All attemps to beat Nature only show the foolish things that a false theory will lead man to do. She cannot be beaetn. We may easily move off and beat our board or rent bills. We may beat our grocery bills, etc., but we cant' beat Nature. She will not be denied. We may move to California, Colorado, we may travel to Europe, but we cannot escape Nature. She goes right along with us wherever we go.

Cures are attributed to various lauded methods of treatment. Now there can be no denying that recovery does often take place under all methods, but there can be some doubts about the curative power of the method. The organism is, as we have shown, a self-curative thing and is capable of putting up a winning fight against great odds.

If the treatment employed must always account for the recovery then experience can easily be made to show that all the millions of absurd and even harmful practices that man has employed in the treatment of disease possessed remarkable healing powers. Again, if the thing done must always account for the results obtained, isn't it just as logical to say when a patient dies: "The patient was sick, he was treated in this way and died, therefore the treatment killed him," as it is to say: "The patient was sick, he was treated in this manner and recovered, therefore the treatment cured him?"

HYGIENE OF CHRONIC DISEASE

Health comes through healthful living and for this there are no substitutes. There can be no substitutes.

I cannot refrain from repeating a story told the class by Professor John W. Sargent, D.P., N.D., then with "The International Health Resort," and "The International College of Drugless Physicians" (Chicago). He stated that he once had a patient under his care in the institution who, being rich and used to being petted, pampered and fussed over, complained that he was not getting enough treatment. To his complaint Dr. Sargent replied: "Why man treatment won't cure you. If it would we would hire three shifts and give you treatment for twenty-four hours a day." The gentleman saw the point and became content with the treatment he was receiving and soon recovered. That treatment won't cure is a truth that is yet to be learned by both the public and the healing professions.

The requirements for recovery from chronic disease do not differ essentially from those required in acute disease. The condition that is forcing the trouble must in all cases be removed. This means that both the immediate and remote occasions for the abnormal action must be removed. Thus our first prescription must be a proscription of those habits and indulgences that are enervating and weakening the patient. A real recovery cannot take place until the enervation is overcome. Stimulating methods may palliate for a time, but palliation is not cure.

Vital recuperation cannot take place as long as the enervating habits are continued. Vital recuperation will be retarded by stimulating methods of treatment. Such recuperation will be hastened by a period of rest. By rest we mean mental, physical and physiological rest.

Nature demands that the disturbing elements be removed. Give the organism an opportunity to cleanse itself and it will eliminate its wastes and free itself of toxins, providing, of course, it has the necessary vitality to do so. If it hasn't sufficient vitality we cannot supply it with this precious force and all our attempts at forcing it to work, by stimulating its activities only weaken it and hasten the end. Such practices only enervate the patient and render the organism less able to return to normal.

The essentials of cure are:—
1 Stop all enervating habits.
2 Stop the absorption of all poisons from the outside.
3 Give the organism an opportunity to recuperate its dissipated force.
4 Supply any element or condition that is required for the comfort of the patient.

"We have found," says Dr. Walter, *Exact Science of Health*, p. 237. "it to be invariable that what makes the man sick is the thing which he never wants to relinquish. Evil habits make for themselves such a place in the organism that it is almost impossible to live without them, and so the patient is willing to do almost anything in order to recover, except the thing which he must do. This would seem to be the chief reason why we have had the greatest success with the most desperate cases. Such a patient is willing at length to submit, and do what is necessary, but the rule is with patients who are only playing sick, to follow your prescriptions as long as they are agreeable, and for the rest evade all requirements."

People will not abandon their pet vices and cherished indulgences until they have reached that point of desperation where they are willing to do anything, even torture themselves, if only they may return to comfort. Those who are not very sick, those who still have hope of cure by methods that do not require correction of cause, are unwilling to forego the injurious habits to which they are enslaved. But Graham truly declared:—

"In chronic diseases, all practice which is not based upon a careful and thorough investigation of the causes, as well as the symptoms of the case, is in fact nothing but downright quackery, and far more frequently does harm than good. For in such practice, the causes of the disease, existing in the dietetic and other voluntary habits of the patient, ARE SUFFERED TO REMAIN AND CONSTANTLY EXERT THEIR MORBIFIC INFLUENCE BY WHICH THE DISEASE WAS ORIGINALLY INDUCED, AND CONTINUES TO BE PERPETUATED. (Caps. mine. Author). Nay, indeed, those very causes are frequently employed as remedial agents to remove the diseases which they have originated and are perpetuating. Thus I have in multitudes of instances seen people who have been severely afflicted for years, by diseases which were principally induced by the habitual use of alcoholic and narcotic substances, and which had been kept alive by the continued use of those substances as medicine; and all that was necessary to remove the diseases and restore the sufferers to health, was to take away their medicine. Again, I have seen instances in which individuals had suffered under the most cruel affections of the heart and head and other parts, and submitted to medical treatment for years without the least relief. Yet on taking away their tea and coffee, which were the principle originating and perpetuating causes of their sufferings, they were soon restored to perfect health. But the practitioner had wholly overlooked or entirely disregarded these causes, and suffered them to keep alive the symptoms which they were combatting with their medicine, and by their medicine rendering their patients only the more morbidly susceptible to the effects of these morbific causes, and I have seen hundreds of miserable dyspeptics who had suffered almost everything for years; scores of those whose symptoms strongly indicated pulmonary consumption, and sometimes apparently in its advanced stage; many who had been for years afflicted with epileptic and other kinds of fits and spasmodic affections, or with cruel asthma, or sick headache; in short, I have seen nearly every form of chronic disease with which the human body is afflicted in civilized life, after resisting almost every kind of medical treatment for years, yield in a very short time to a correct diet and well regulated general regimen. And why was all this? Because, in almost every case, the disease had been originated and perpetuated by dietetic errors; and the practitioners had been unsuccessful, because with all their administration of medicine, they had suffered these dietetic errors to remain undisturbed, unquestioned —nay, perhaps even recommended."—*Science of Human Life*, p. 437.

So long as man believes in cures and immunizers he will continue to search for these things and ignore the real causes of his trouble. How do men expect to cure the effects of coffee drinking while they continue drinking coffee? How do they expect to cure these effects of coffee drinking by drinking more coffee? Such expectations are not worthy reasoning beings, whether it is coffee, alcohol, sexual abuses, gluttony or other evil habits.

Graham truly declared:—

"It ought, furthermore to be understood that ALL MEDICINE AS SUCH, IS IN ITSELF AN EVIL; that its own direct effect on the living body is in all cases, without exception, unfriendly to life; and the action of all medicine, as such, in every case, to a greater or less extent wears out life, impairs the constitution and abbreviates the period of human existence. To throw an immense quantity of medicine into the diseased body, and accidentally kill or cure, as the event may happen to be, requires but little science or skill; and extensive experience has taught us that it may be done as well by the acknowledge quack as by the licensed physician: but to understand all the properties, powers, laws, and relations of the living body, so well as to be able to stand by it in the moment of disease, and, as it were, to look through it at a glance, and detect its morbid affections and actions, and ascertain its morbific causes, and to know how to guide and regulate the energies of life in accordance with its own laws, in such a manner as to remove obstructions, relieve oppressions, subdue diseased actions, and restore health, with little or no medicine, but principly or entirely by a regimen wisely adapted to the case, evinces the most profound skill; and such qualifications are essential to the character of the truly enlightened and philanthropic physician: and such physicians truly deserve the support and respect and admiration and love of every member of society, as standing among the highest benefactors of the human family."—*Science of Human Life*, p. 425.

Again:—

"We see, therefore, that the essential elements of health are the healthy condition and functions of the organs of the body; and these elements are preserved by a strict conformity to the laws of constitution and relation established in our nature, and they are destroyed or impaired by every infraction of those laws. And such are the sympathies of the system, that not only are the organs immediately acted on by disturbing and morbific causes themselves affected and their function deranged and diseased by such causes, but other organs also, sympathizing with those immediately acted on by those causes, partake of their irritations, and by these sympathetic irritations, are often made themselves the seats of local disease; and when disease is thus once induced, even slight habitual disturbances and irritations from dietetic errors and other causes are sufficient to keep it up for many years, till it terminates perhaps in death.

"We see, also, that no physician, nor any other human being in the universe, can come to us when we are diseased, and by any exercise of skill or the application of any remedy, directly and immediately impart to us any health, or remove from us any disease. But the truly enlightenend, scientific, and skillful physician, is generally, able to discover the nature of our disease, and to ascertain what disturbing causes must be removed, and what means must be employed in order to the restoration of healthy action and condition of every organ and part, and thus, by assisting nature's own renovating and healing economy, relieve the system from disease, and enable it to return to health.***

"All that nature asks, or can receive, from human skill, in such a condition, therefore, is the removal of disturbing causes; and she will, of her own accord, as naturally as a stone falls to the earth, return to health, unless the vital constitution has received an irreparable injury.—*Science of Human Life*, p. 424-5.

Lastly:—

"The only aid, therefore, that human skill and science can afford the diseased body in recovering health, is, with strict regard to the physiological properties and laws of the system, to assist it, so far as possible, in throwing off oppressions, removing obstructions and all irritating causes, and in subduing irritations, and restoring healthy action and function. And in order to do this, it is requisite, in the first place, that the physician should well understand the physiological powers and laws of the body; in the second place, that he should understand the nature of the disease; and in the third place, as a general rule, that he should fully and clearly ascertain the cause of the disease. For, as Hippocrates justly observes, the man who attempts to cure a disorder without knowing the cause, is like a blind man or one groping in the dark,—he is as likely to do harm as good."—*Science of Human Life*, p. 436.

Let me caution you against alarm from the immediate and apparently depressing effects which are unavoidable when one suddenly gives up any long-continued violation of physical law. There is not the slightest danger to health and life in the total, final and sudden abandonment of all wrong doing, of whatever kind, complexity or degree, and no danger in leaving the system to pass through the subsequent renovation and recover itself from the effects of any cause or causes, however depressing, painful or difficult this renovating process may be.

It is in vain to look for gradual emancipation from confirmed habits and transgressions. Tobacco, coffee, tea, alcohol, opium, etc., keep alive the craving for their use. Those who attempt to "taper off" usually end up in failure to break their bondage and free themselves.

The morbid desire for these substances is kept alive by the least indulgence in them. There is no safety for the user until the morbid irritability of the nervous system is overcome and normal *sensibility* is restored. The least quantity that the organic instincts can appreciate is sufficient to forever prolong the morbid condition of the nervous system; and, until the nervous system is restored to a normal state, the user is not safe for an instant. Until then the smell of tobacco, for instance, sight of a cigar or even the thought or mention of tobacco may revive the morbid craving with almost irresistable force. The habit will be overcome with greater ease and much less suffering if broken off at once.

The blood is poisoned even by small amounts of these substances. Take alcohol as an instance. If one attempts to "taper off" on its use, and while continuing its use, daily uses a little less, he is still daily taking into his system the poison and is being injured even by these amounts. Absolute abstinence from the start will lessen the suffering incident to overcoming the practice.

Sexual excitation and gratification are of the same character. The more the sex function is excited and gratified, the more it demands of these. "The artificial and varied repetition of sexual excitation," says Forel, "by means of objects which provoke it, increases the sexual appetite." When habitual mental and mechanical excitation of the sexual organs have produced in them a morbid condition which demands frequent "gratification" every repetition of the excitation serves to perpetuate the condition.

What is true of tobacco, alcohol, sex, etc., is equally true of other excitants or irritants, such as condiments,—salt, pepper, spices,—opium, cathartics, mechanical irritants, etc.

As soon as the sources of irritation and waste of organic power are corrected and removed, so that there is no longer any need of power to combat the irritation and the power usually wasted in various dissipations is conserved, there follows a reduced determination of nervous energies to these points and an increased amount of energy is devoted to the more important work of cleansing and repairing the damaged organism. The organs of elimination are reinforced to enable them to eliminate what Jennings called "the arrearages of expurgation that have accumulated in consequence of their having been overtaxed."

Make up your mind to abandon these things once and for all—not one at a time, not by some miscalled transition program, but abruptly, and all at once. Have it over with. Go through the pain, discomfort and depression all at once and be sure that you will suffer less than by the tapering off method. Your recovery will be more rapid, more sure and more satisfactory.

"What would be the result" asks Jennings "of a sudden and universal cessation of hostilities against the vital economy, throughout the length and bredth of the land? Imagination would fail to draw a picture equal to the reality.

"Nature would hold a jubilee."

The *Law of Limitation* would immediately withdraw all forces from the former points of attack and begin the work of renovating the system. A depressed, irritable, languid people with frequent cases of *delirium tremens*, many aching heads, and shaking limbs would be the immediate result. But the ultimate outcome would be a happy issue. Improved health and strength, clearer minds and more cheerful dispositions would result

MENTAL INFLUENCES: The mind should be poised, worry, anxiety, grief, anger, jealousy, self-pity, irritableness, etc., should be avoided as far as possible. Fears of all kinds should be put out of the mind. Hope, faith, confidence, cheer and courage should dominate the mind of the recovering sick man or woman. Relatives, friends, and all those around the sick should offer all the encouragement possible. This they often fail to do. On the contrary these often do all they can, although, not wilfully, to prevent recovery.

Nothing can so effectively illustrate the self-reliant vitality and inherent truthfulness of the hygienic practice than the manner in which it daily and hourly triumphs over great obstacles. We are forced to meet and overcome the ingrown prejudices, blind adherence to age-long traditions, morbid feelings and artificial appetences, not alone of our patients, but also of their relatives, friends and former physicians. The impertinent intermeddlings of the patient's friends, the insolent machinations of their have-been and would-be physicians, the dogged and persistent opposition of members of their families, renders the problem of caring for a sick person by the hygienic method a delicate and trying one.

This ignorant opposition and malicious meddling on the part of relatives, friends and physicians is more effective when the patients are in their home than when they are in a hygienic institution. Sometimes it is a drugged-to-death wife, at other times a drugged-to-death husband who is anxious to try the hygienic system, but who finds it impossible to do so at home because of unreasoning interference and determined meddling. I have seen patients who were so harrassed and annoyed by members of their family because such patients dared attempt to get well through hygiene, after drugs had failed, that they were made worse, and, often such patients do not get better until they get away from home and the hurtful psychology of friend and relative.

The technically professional part of our practice is the easiest part. Our most difficult work is that of overcoming and counteracting the traditions and habits of society, the ignorance and perjudices of the patient, the feelings and opinions of friends and relatives and insolent machinations of physicians. It often seems that every one around the patient is doing all in his or her power to prevent recovery. So true is this that I often think that the first thing a sick man or woman should do who is going to attempt to get well hygienically, at home, is to get a good club and empty the house of everyone except himself or herself.

"Fasting will kill you." "You are too thin now." "You are not strong enough to fast." "You will never come out of it alive." "I should be afraid to risk it." "Fasting is good in some *cases*, but—but, very dangerous in others." "Your stomach will get so it cannot take food." These and similar encouraging exclamations and dogmatic statements are offered by relatives, friends and physicians, to cheer up those sick men and women, who disparing of help from poisonous pills, plasters, powders and potions and from knives and saws, are about to embark on a hygienic ship for a voyage to the land of health. Well meaning, but misguided and unthinking members of one's own family are frequently guilty of such discouraging and disheartening suggestions. I have heard them fall repeatedly from the lips of those who pretend a knowledge of psychology and who should know the evil wrought by such suggestions.

"Your doctor is starving you to death!" "You are looking terribly bad!" "There is no color in your cheeks and you are losing weight!" "This diet may be alright for some cases, but you need plenty of good nourishing food." "You need to be built up."

If you were sick and on an eliminating diet and your system was being cleaned out, and due to lack of its accustomed stimulation your body did look bad, and some one hurled a barrage like the above at you, wouldn't it depress you and actually make you worse? And if it came from your whole family and all your friends day in and day out would you expect to get well? If you knew you were on the right track and felt your relatives and friends were either ignorant or stubborn or both and you became irritated or angry at their opposition to what you were doing, and fought back, would you expect to be able to digest your food?

If you quarreled with them and then cried and finally became hysterical would you not expect to have headaches, pains and gas in the abdomen, weakness and other throubles? Just these things, I have seen in many cases. Only those of strong wills and strong convictions can pass through such a barrage of evil influences as frequently come from family, friends and physicians, and recover in spite of the efforts of these to prevent recovery. A man's enemies are of his own household. His best friends are often his worst foes.

CLEANLINESS:—This is essential both locally and generally. To effect this, simple bathing in plain water at a moderate temperature is sufficient. Hot and cold baths should never be resorted to. The nearer the temperature of the water approaches that of the body the less of an excitant it is, the less it shocks the body and the less energy is wasted in resisting it. Luke warm or slightly cool baths, as often as needed, may be employed. One does not always require a daily bath.

Stay in the water only so long as is required to cleanse the body. Do not soak yourself. Get out as quickly as possible and dry off with a coarse towel. Vigorously rub the body with this.

Years ago the author fell victim to the cold bathing fad. Each morning he had his cold bath, even breaking the ice and going in on more than one occasion. Such a bath is a powerful stimulant, if one does not remain in the water too long, and has sufficient reactive power. But by so much as it stimulates at first it also depresses later. It is an enervating practice with not the shadow of an excuse for existence. I would strongly caution everyone against such foolish practices.

"The end of the day," says Dr. Owald, "is the best time for a sponge bath; a sponge and a coarse towel have often cured insomnia when diacodium failed. A bucketful of tepid water will do for ordinary purposes; daily cold shower-baths in winter time are as preposterous as hot drinks in the dog-days. Russian baths and ice water cures owe their repute to the same popular delusion that ascribes miraculous virtues to nauseating drugs—the mistrust of our natural instincts, culminating in the idea that all natural things must be injurious to man, and that the efficacy of a remedy depends on the degree of its repulsiveness. Ninety-nine boys in a hundred would rather take the bitterest medicine than a cold bath in mid-winter. If we leave children and animals to the guidance of their instincts they will become amphibious in the dog-days, and quench their thirst at the coldest spring without fear of injurious consequences; but in winter time even wild beasts avoid emersion with an instinctive dread. A Canadian bear will make a wide circuit or pick his way over the floes, rather than swim a lake in cold weather. Baptist missionaries do not report many revivals before June. Warm springs, on the other hand, attract all birds and beasts that stay with us in winter time; the hot spas of Rockport, Arkansas, are visited nightly by raccoons and foxes in spite of all torch-light hunts; and Haxthausen tells us that in hard winters the thermae of Pactigorsk, in the eastern Caucasus, attracts dear and wild hogs from the distant Rerek Valley. I know the claims of the hydropathic school, and the arguments pro and con, but the main points of the controversy still hinge upon the issue between Nature's testimony and Dr. Priessnitz's."—*Physical Eductaion*, p. 100-1.

THE FRICTION BATH: This consists in going over the body with the hands, or with a towel or a flesh brush, or the friction mittens and thorougly rubbing every part of it. It is an excellent means of cleansing and invigorating the skin. Care should be used not to rub hard enough to injure and peel the skin. This should be taken daily.

THE SUN BATH: Some diseases like anemia, rickets, tuberculosis, leukemia, scrofula, psoriasis, etc., do not get well without sunlight. It is of distinct value in all chronic conditions. A daily sun bath should be had whenever possible.

THE AIR BATH: Just what effect the air has on the skin, and nerves in the skin is not well known but it is known to benefit these. A daily air bath should be had. This may be had at the same time the sun bath is taken. The friction bath may also accompany these.

EXERCISE: Many cases of chronic disease are largely due to a lack of physical exercise. Thousands have regained their health by doing little more than taking up systematic physical exercise.

In all cases of chronic disease where no condition of the joints, muscles, heart, lungs, kidneys, or elsewhere, contraindicate it, daily physical exercise should be indulged. This should be mild at first and should be increased both in amount and vigor as returning strength permits.

In diseases of the heart, hardening of the arteries, advanced diseases of the lungs, inflammation and tuberculosis of the joints, and similar conditions, exercise must be indulged in very cautiously and moderately.

In dropsical conditions, advanced Bright's disease, etc., it is usually advisable to take no exercise at all, until the condition is greatly improved. Inflamed and tuberculous joints should not be exercised. They should be given perfect rest.

REST: "Rest and replenishment of power," says Jennings, "is the first step in the ascending pathological transit; removal of useless matter by the decomposing function, with its activity and force increased by resting, constitutes the second step, and the third consists in a repair of breaches. These three steps form the first grand division in the ascending pathological transition, the removal of *structural* derangement, or cure of organic disease. The next grand step in the ascending pathological work consists in the re-establishment of regular or natural *functional* action."—*Philosophy of Human Life*, p. 102.

Neither functional nor structural derangement can be remedied except by the reinforcement of appropriate power and this can only come when all the waste-gates are closed and recuperation through rest is secured.

The path of professional duty in plain. Point out the importance of strict regard to economy in the expenditure of organic funds, that they may be brought so far within the income and accumulate, that nature may be able to liquidate her debts, and get above board again, before she is thrown into other and more embarrassing straits.

In most cases of chronic disease, a prolonged period in bed, say from three to six weeks, and longer in many cases, constitutes the speediest means of recovery. The individual should go to bed, reconcile himself to it and remain there as long as is necessary for full recuperation.

Some mild exercise, unless this is contraindicated, should be taken each day or twice each day during the period in bed.

The mind should be set at ease so that mental rest is secured.

Where it is not possible to get away from one's work and rest, as above described, one should cut down his daily mental, physical and physiological activities, as far as this is possible, and secure as much rest and sleep each day as circumstances will permit. Go to bed at the earliest possible hour. Remain in bed as late in the morning as possible. Rest during the day if this can be arranged. Where this can be done it is well to lie down for a half hour to two hours and rest and sleep, if possible, in the afternoon.

Amusement, excitement, stimulation, late hours, etc., should all be avoided in every possible way. The conservation of energy in every way this can be done is desirable. The more one can rest the more rapid and more satisfactory will be his recovery.

SLEEP: Invalids and chronic sufferers generally do not get enough sleep. The importance of sound, quiet and sufficient sleep cannot be overestimated. It is during sleep chiefly that structures are repaired. Recuperation reaches its maximum of efficiency during sleep.

The rule for invalids and chronic sufferers is: RETIRE EARLY AND REMAIN IN BED AS LONG AS YOU CAN SLEEP QUIETLY.

The bedding should be as hard, and the bed-clothing as light as a due regard for comfort will permit. A hot jug to the feet will assure warmth if the weather is cold. If one is chilled he does not sleep.

Heavy meals, indigestible and stimulating foods, stimulating beverages, as tea, coffee, cocoa, chocolate, alcohol, soda fountain drinks, etc., and all drugs should be avoided, as these prevent sound, restful sleep. If sleep is inclined to be restless, vapory and dreamy during the nights, the evening meal may be omitted.

Do not sleep on pillows. Avoid all crooked bodily positions. Relax the body and mind as fully as possible . If sleep does not come immediately do not fuss and fume over it. Worry will keep you awake. Do not roll and toss in bed. This will exhaust you. Lie still and rest. Do not get up and walk the floor. Relax and rest, you'll go to sleep much quicker. Don't try to go to sleep. The effort will keep you awake. Don't resort to any kind of sleep producers or any sleep inducing procedures, however harmless these may appear to be.

Have your bed room well ventilated. Flood it with sunshine during the day. Whenever possible sleep out doors.

SLEEPLESSNESS: This, declares Page, "is often referred to as a cause of insanity, but it would be much nearer the truth to say that insanity causes sleeplessness

"To attack insomnia as a disease instead of a symptom, is sure to result in discomfiture, in the great majority of cases and is in every instance unsound in principle.*** A man is wakeful at night because under his present physical condition he ought to be—just as in diarrhea, the looseness is doing its work of cure.*** Let him know that sleeplessness is an analogue of pain, and he will, or may, bear it philosophically, and thus tend to its removal.

"But, thinking all the while that it is sleep only that he needs, his sleeplessness distresses him, causes him to be more and more alarmed, and, consequently, has the effect to postpone the oblivion so devoutly prayed for, but so little earned. To *deserve* sleep is to have it."—*The Natural Cure,* pp. 133-4-5.

One should lie down after a half-hour of quiet and freedom from exciting mental exercise and then, when he draws the covers over him, it should be with a sublime indifference as to whether he shall or shall not fall asleep immediately. Resort to no sleep producers. Those efforts at subduing the senses, such as attempts to shut out external impressions by closing the eyes, stopping the ears and lowering the sensibilities generally, are frequently the causes of persistent wakefulness. Efforts to go to sleep by repeating metaphysical formulas are fruitless and often keep one awake. Any exercise of the higher mental faculties will tend to keep one awake. One remains awake because he tries to go to sleep. To *endeavour* to go to sleep is a mistake.

Narcotics or sleeping-draughts do not produce sleep, but stupor. Their use is both irrational and injurious, and if long continued, fatal. They produce a worse form of sleeplessness than that for which they are given.

Go to bed, relax, let go—do not roll and toss on the bed, do not get up and walk the floor, do not worry and fret—and calmly await sleep. Let your eyelids finally droop in sleep because you are truly sleepy. Every effort to force sleep keeps you awake and prevents both mind and body from resting.

Cut out your coffee, tobacco and other stimulants and earn your sleep. Then, and not until then, will you have normal sleep.

CRISES: Even the strongest Heteropath will usually concede that when the symptoms of a disease are obviously improving, the action is *right action*—but when the symptoms appear to be growing worse, he will insist that the action is *wrong action*. He conceives disease as a "pulling down" process. A woman who was under Dr. Jennings' care for a chronic affection of the lungs developed several crises—"there would be a gradual improvement in the general symptoms for two or three months, and then a sudden falling back of them, attended by spitting of blood, pain and soreness about the chest, with diminution of appetite and strength, and depression of spirits"—said to him on one occasion: "I am satisfied that on the whole I am gaining, and were it not for these running down turns, I should feel very much encouraged." The doctor replied:—

"You greatly misconceive of these things to which you give the appelation of 'running down.' They are *running up* turns.' A feeble team in ascending a long hill finds it necessary to stop and rest a little occasionally to recruit its strength. You gain more in those days when you feel the worse, so far as acquisition or treasuring up of your vital energy is concerned than you do in three weeks when you feel the best. The machine exhausts its power, runs down its weight and these are the winding up spells.

"It costs comparatively little to sustain the vital operations when you feel the worst, and it is simply because there is but little energy expended on the complaining parts that they do thus complain. The income of power continues the same now that is was under the free distribution of it, and while the law of limitation is in force, and you have, consequently, no muscular power to exercise with, be contented to keep still."—*Medical Reform*, p. 341.

Do not expect nature to go forward in a steady, uniform and undeviating course. In difficult cases, and cases of low vitality, she must have her resting spells. During these periods the symptoms will appear from the Heteropathic view, unfavorable. Appetite will fag. The pulse will grow weak. The patient will feel weak, tired, depressed. Sores will look bad, the breath will become foul. There will be an increase in all or most of the symptoms. Acute symptoms may develop. The invalid, that previously seemed to be improving, now seems to be growing worse.

These crises are to be handled just as all acute conditions are handled. Above all the invalid should avoid becoming discouraged or frightened when these appear. Welcome them and rejoice in the improved health which follows them.

FITS: "Instead of fits tending to the destruction of life, they tend to its preservation; and indeed, are as absolutely necessary, in some cases, for the eking out of life, as the repairs of a ship, every day thumped against the rocks, are for its salvation. No man ever died by a fit; and when a man dies in a fit his life is prolonged somewhat by it."—*Medical Reform*, p. 145.

THE BOWELS: These are usually a source of much worry and annoyance, due to the persistent propaganda kept up by those who have constipation cures for sale. Dire consequences are pictured as sure to follow if one does not have one or more bowel movements daily. Constipation, or intestinal stasis, as it is now known, is not the real source of evil. It is an effect.

"Intestinal stasis" is the reaction from overaction. Or, to put this more simply, it is a period of rest of the bowels following overwork of the bowels, or of the body as a whole. As soon as they have had sufficient rest for recuperation, the bowels, will act if there is need for action. Hysterical, impatient dupes of the medical bund grab a pill or a bottle as soon as their bowels fail to act, and give them the lash.

The drugs, being powerful irritants, occasion rapid, forceful contractions of the muscles of the stomach, intestines and colon, and the pouring out of large quantities of secretions to wash away the irritant drug. The dupes of such practices secure the bowel action they desire, but at frightful cost. There is now greater need for rest than before the drug was taken. There is now less of the normal lubricants of the intestine and bowel than before. There must, of necessity, be a longer period of rest following such violent activity. But the rest is not allowed. Another dose of the drug is taken, resulting in another period of overwork, necessitating more rest. This process keeps up, until chronic constipation results and, if it goes on, permanent weakness, and ultimately, atrophy of the muscles and glands of these organs, with a thickening and hardening of their lining membranes and derangement of secretion.

There are many ways of forcing increased action in debiliated organs, for a brief period, providing there is enough power in reserve to supply the action, but these things always and necessarily diminish the power of that action and do so in precisely the degree to which they accelerate the action. The increase of action is occasioned by the extra expenditure of power called out, not supplied, by the compulsory process, and therefore this quantity of power is diminished by this amount. This is a needless and criminal waste. For the power is wanted for other purposes and will be used more judiciously and advantageously by the undisturbed law of appropriation and distribution of the living system.

Few people realize how much time and money they really spend trying to cover up evidences of their ill health instead of improving their health. If they are constipated, they blame the constipation for their ill health instead of blaming the impairment of their health for the constipation. This leads them to try to improve their health by using cathartics and laxatives to force their bowels to act, instead of overcoming their constipation by improving their health. Constipation is an effect, a symptom—they regard is as a cause.

If they have a filthy mouth, they regard this as the cause of their ill health, instead of the ill health as the cause of the filthy mouth. A healthy mouth is a clean mouth. A healthy breath is a sweet breath. All of the orifices and cavities of man's body are sweet and clean so long as they are in a state of health. None of the excretions of man's body are offensive if he is truly healthy. If the sweat from your body smells offensively it is an evidence of disease. If your breath is offensive instead of being sweet, you are sick. If your mouth is dirty, you are diseased.

But don't persist in your habit of getting the cart before the horse. An unclean mouth is not the cause of disease. It is an effect—a symptom. You don't improve your health by scrubbing your teeth, rinsing your mouth, and gargling your throat. These remedy nothing. Good health is the best mouth wash, the best tooth brush, the best laxative, and the best deodorant. Get Health First and all these things will be added unto you.

Every organ in man's body acts automatically and to its own and the body's best interests. Every opening or cavity of the body which opens upon the outside world is self-cleansing. The eyes are self-cleansing. The nose, mouth, ears, bowels, vagina, etc., are each and all self-cleansing. The normal secretions of all the cavities and orifices of the body are antiseptic and the normal condition of all these cavities and oricfies is aseptic.

A healthy mouth is a clean mouth. A healthy alimentary canal is a clean canal. It is health that produces a clean canal, and not a clean canal that produces health. These organs are supplied with an adequate means of cleansing themselves, and it is astonishing with what promptness and thoroughness they do their work when they have sufficient power. When enervation has impaired secretion and nutrition, so that there is a depravation of the secretions of the intestine and bowel, then these cavities may become septic. Bacterial decomposition sets in and poisons are generated.

Whether these poisons will be absorbed or not will depend on a number of things. Absorption may occur in the small intestine where resistance is not great, but the colon is largely an *excreting* and not a *secreting* organ and much absorption can only occur when it is forced by obstruction. It can never occur if motive power is abundant, for the decomposing food will be sent out of the system too quickly for this. We should work for good health, and then all the organs and functions of the body will take care of themselves.

Bowel action is automatic like the pulsations of the heart and the rythmic motions of the chest in breathing. If the power of motions is present and there is need of a movement a movement there will be. If there is need of a rest due to deficiency of power the bowels will rest. They may be goaded to action by drugs, enemas, rectal dilators, spinal stimulation, etc., but this only makes their condition worse. The best plan is to let them alone and permit them to attend to their own business.

"But doctor, aren't you going to do anything to make my bowels move?" asked a young lady of me once.

I replied: "your bowels do not require to be made to move any more than your heart needs to be made to beat or your lungs to breathe. The trouble with your bowels now is that they have been made to move too much, already."

This lady whose age was about twenty, had taken laxatives and cathartics every day of her life from infancy. We let her wait upon nature. On the thirteenth day her bowels moved, and in a few days they were moving twice a day on two meals a day. This has continued for two years, even continuing throughout the entire length of one pregnancy.

Two movements a day on two meals a day is normal. These movements should not require more than five to ten seconds to completely empty the bowels and should be accompanied with a distinctly pleasurable sensation. They should be absolutely free of all odor. No effort is required in normal bowel action. No straining and grunting is necessary. The movement is so easy and so quickly over that one hardly realizes he has had a bowel movement.

I have let numbers of cases run from ten to fourteen days in order to let their bowels move spontaneously. This they always do and after they once begin to move they continue to do so. Never once have I seen any harm result from this procedure. Indeed in every case there has been a steady improvement in health. As instances, one case that went thirteen days made the following improvements—temperature which had been 101° F., became normal, tongue cleared up, fetid breath became normal, rapid heart became normal, strength returned so that the patient could get out of bed and headaches ceased. All of this before the bowels moved. Another case, one that required fourteen days of waiting before the bowels moved made the following improvements—pimples that covered his face healed up, yellowish cast to white portions of the eyes cleared up and he grew stronger. A diabetic patient who had been running .4% to .2% sugar in the urine under medical care and who showed .3% upon beginning my instructions, showed no sugar from the seventh day on and grew stronger during the time.

Dr. Page says: "Tanner had no movement during his fast (40 days); Griscomb's experience was similar, and Connolly, the consumptive who fasted forty-three days, had no movement for three weeks."

Dr. Page, who opposed the employment of laxatives, cathartics, enamas, laxative foods etc, for the purpose of "curing constipation," saying that if there has been no action for two, three or even four days, it need occasion no alarm, and the novice will be surprised to see how natural a movement will finally reward his or her patience in awaiting her call, instead of badgering her into unusual activity, declares:—

"A good rule for many who suffer tortures of mind because of constipation would be: mind your own business and let your bowels mind theirs. Strive not to *have* movements, but rather to *deserve* them. That is, attend to the general health by living hygienically, and the bowels will, if given *regular opportunity*, move when there is anything to move for."

Again:—

"In common life, it is rare indeed that constipation is the result of a deficient diet, although it often arises from lack of nourishment consequent upon excess, or an unwholesome variety of food, or both. Usually it may be regarded as the 'reaction' from over-action. The not uncommon experience, in regular order, is this: Excess in diet, diarrhea, constipation, physic or enema, purgation, worse constipation, more physic and so on. The term reaction here means simply that the organs involved having been irritated by undigested food, and having by means of increased action cleared away the obstructions, now seek restoration by the most natural method, as the name itself implies—rest. What are commonly called diseases are in reality cures; and the common practice with drug doctors, of controlling the symptoms is like answering the cries of a drowning man with a knock on the head."—*The Natural Cure*, p. 112.

It is well known that the effects of all laxative and cathartic drugs "wear out." The size of the dose must frequently be increased and the drug must occasionally be exchanged for a different one. But it is not generally understood that laxative foods also "wear out." One must eat more and more of them; even then they will finally cease to occasion action. Eating quantities of "roughage" or "bulk" will not cure constipation. *Of more importance than the thing to be moved (the bulk) is the motive power—the power of movement.* Constipation is due to enervation and will end when this is corrected and its causes removed. Keep in mind that *it is good health that insures daily movements and not daily movements that insure good health.*

We might just as well attempt to escape the law of dual effect as to try to escape the secondary effect of forcing bowel action with laxative foods. As Page truly says:—

"Next to the mistake of resorting to drugs in these cases, is the quite common one of swallowing special kinds of food for the same purpose, and there is some question as to which of the two evils is the least. An excessive quantity of rye mush, wheaten grits, or oat groats, with a generous dressing of butter, syrup, milk, or honey to wash it down in abnormal haste, will often purge the bowels like the most drastic poison."—*The Natural Cure*, p. 114.

Olive oil, wheat bran, agar agar, etc., taken for the same purpose are no better than drugs.

Dr. Gibson has admirably expressed this same thought in his "*Facts and Fancies in "Health Foods."* He says:—

"To most dietitians the main object of diet seems to be to prepare such food-mixtures as increase intestinal peristalsis. This, however is a misconception of the real value of diet. As there are two ways of increasing the activity of your horse, so there are two ways of stimulating a sluggish bowel: by whipping or feeding. The one is irritation, the other nutrition; and to stimulate a system into a physiological heightening of its activities, without impairing a corresponding amount of nourishment is no less ridiculous than the notion that a worn-out horse can be strenghtened by a freely applied whip.

"Peristalsis is due to a wave of nervous energy, arising in the semilunar ganglia and solar plexus, from which center the ensuing momentum is dispensed throughout the intestinal coil. The process resembles the mechanical movement of a watch in which the wheels receive their impulse from the movement generated in the static, high-tensioned power of the coiled-up mainspring. And, futhermore, just as in the case of a weakened mainspring, the watch may occasionally be made to move up to the correct time by an appropriate manipulation of its hands and wheels, so intestinal peristalsis may be temporarily regulated by mechanical or chemical irritation, due to coarse, indigestible food-stuff, while in reality not a single momentum of vital energy may have been added to the nerve life of the organism."

With equal truth the doctor might have added that the stimulation of intestinal peristalsis actually robs the organism of part of its "nerve life." For, as he truly observes on another page: "an agent which has the power to move the bowels yet does not possess the vital elements necessary for the regeneration of the weakened nerve power, in place of adding energy to the organism becomes a positive loss to its reserves."

WATER DRINKING: Thirst should be the guide in this matter. Drink only when thirsty and drink enough to satisfy thirst. But be sure it is true thirst and not merely irritation from salt, condiments and the like. Much damage is done to invalids by excessive water drinking taken with a view of increasing elimination.

FASTING: In chronic disease a fast is not always essential. Indeed, it is seldom necessary. Recovery may be brought about in most cases merely by limiting the diet as previously indicated. However this will require more time than if a fast is employed. A short fast of from three to ten days, and longer in many csaes, will be found beneficial in practically every case. Indeed, it is possible in most cases to continue the fast until all or nearly all the symptoms of the disease have disappeared and health is re-established. This has been done in thousands of cases.

DIET: Graham declares: "The question is, how to remove all irritations from the system, and restore each part to healthy action and condition. But almost all the articles of medicine, not excepting those called tonics, are either directly or indirectly irritating or debilitating in their effects on the living body, and therefore should be avoided as far as possible. Many of the articles of diet ordinarily used in civilized life are also decidedly irritating and pernicious; and many of the modes of preparing food, are sources of irritation to the system. In fact, when the body is seriously diseased, even the necessary functions of alimentation, under the very best regimen, are, to a considerable extent, the sources of irritation; and where it is possible to sustain life without nutrition, entire and protracted fasting would be the very best means in many cases of removing disease and restoring health. I have seen wonderful effects result from experiments of this kind."—*Science of Human Life*.

After controverting the opinion that fleshiness and the muscular power of the body are to be considered as criteria of the excellence of any regimen prescribed for the chronic invalid, and pointing out that to eat increases the pain, inflammation, discomfort, fever and irritableness of the system, and does so in proportion to the amount of food eaten and in direct ratio to its supposed nutritive qualities, and that to fast or to consume non-irritating, non-stimulating foods and drinks in moderation reduces the "violence" of the disease and renders recovery more certain, he says, (p. 441):—

"Nevertheless, the chronic invalid himself, and generally his friends, and sometimes also his physician, seem to think that fleshiness and muscular strength are the things mainly to be desired and sought for, and that any prescribed regimen is more or less correct and salutary in proportion as it is conducive to these ends. Whereas if they were properly enlightened, they would know that THE MORE THEY NOURISH A BODY WHILE DISEASED ACTION IS KEPT UP IN IT, THE MORE THEY INCREASE THE DISEASE. THE GRAND, PRIMARY OBJECT TO BE AIMED AT BY THE INVALID, IS TO OVERCOME AND REMOVE DISEASED ACTION AND CONDITION, AND RESTORE ALL PARTS TO HEALTH, and THEN nourish the body with a view to fleshiness and strength, AS FAST AS THE FEEBLEST PARTS OF THE SYSTEM WILL BEAR WITHOUT BREAKING DOWN AGAIN. (Capitals mine. Author.) And the regimen best adapted to remove the diseased action and condition, more frequently than otherwise, causes a diminution of flesh and muscular strength (Please note, it is only muscular strength that is diminished. Author's note.), while the disease remains, in regulating the general function of nutrition to the ability of the diseased part. But when the diseased action ceases, and healthy action takes place, the same regimen perhaps will increase the flesh and strength as rapidly as the highest welfare of the constitution will admit." This latter increase in weight and strength on the same regimen would not be possible if the previous loss of fless and strength on it represented an actual loss of vital power. Yet every experienced orthopath knows that what Graham here says is true. The common practice of suffing the chronic sufferer, like a harvest hand is evil. It is even bad for the harvest hand, but is much worse for the invalid. Graham disposed of this practice as follows:—

"In regulating the diet of chronic patients, however, it should always be remembered that the extensiveness and suddenness of any change should correspond with the physiological and pathological condition, and circumstances of the individual; and most especially should it be remembered that the DISEASED ORGAN OR PART SHOULD BE MADE THE STANDARD OF THE ABILITY OF THE SYSTEM. If the boiler of a steam engine is powerful enough in some parts to bear a pressure of fifty pounds to the square inch, while in some other parts it can only bear ten pounds to the square inch, we know that it would not do for the engineer to make the strongest parts of the boiler the standard of its general ability or power, and to attempt to raise a pressure of forty pounds to the square inch, because some parts can bear fifty pounds; for in such an attempt he would surely burst the boiler at its weakest parts. He must therefore make the weakest parts the standard of the general power of the boiler, and only raise such a pressure of steam as those parts can safely bear. SO HE

HYGIENE OF CHRONIC DISEASE

WHO HAS DISEASED LUNGS OR LIVER OR ANY OTHER PART, WHILE AT THE SAME TIME HE HAS A VIGOROUS STOMACH, MUST NOT REGULATE THE QUALITY AND QUANTITY OF HIS FOOD BY THE ABILITY OF HIS STOMACH, BUT BY THE ABILITY OF THE DISEASED PART. This rule is of the utmost importance to the invalid, and one which cannot be disregarded with impunity, and yet it is continually and almost universally violated. Few things are more common than to find individuals who are laboring under severe chronic disease, indulging in very improper qualities and quantities of food, and other dietetic errors, and still strongly contending for the propriety of their habits and practices, on the ground that 'their stomachs never trouble, them.' Alas! They know not that the stomach is the principle source of all their troubles; yet by adopting a correct regimen, and strictly adhering to it for a short time, they would experience such a mitigation of their sufferings, if not such a restoration to health, as would fully convince them of THE SERIOUS IMPROPRIETY OF MAKING A COMPARATIVELY VIGOROUS STOMACH THE STANDARD OF THE PHYSIOLOGICAL ABILITY OF A SYSTEM OTHERWISE DISEASED." (Capitals mine. Author.)—*Science of Human Life*, p. 440.

It is often a difficult task to feed an invalid with a diseased or depraved stomach. A really healthy stomach knows when it has had enough and is fully satisfied with this amount. Its powers of discrimination are strong, the speediness with which it resents any and all injurious or irritating substances, remarkable. It is able to digest any food it may be called upon to digest, and so long as it is treated with fair consideration will never let you know that you have a stomach.

Dr. Jennings rightly said that when "nervous power is supplied in full measur to the ready, obedient workmen; the gastric juice is poured forth abundantly and of good quality, and the important work of digestion is done up in the best manner, and in the shortest time. In this case there is a double guaranty against the unfortunate. occurrence of a fermentative or putrefactive change in the food, which would send forth sharp, irritating gases, accompanied with sour belchings, acrid eructations, heart burns, gastric pains, and a hoast of other dyspeptic difficulties."—*Philosophy of Human Life*, p. 51.

The human stomach is possessed of remarkable powers of adaptation, being able, if supplied with sufficient nerve force, to digest any nutritious substance in any climate, season, altitude, and under almost any circumstance of life; is capable of performing a large amount of labor; is content with a very small allowance of food, or will patiently abstain entirely from all food for a long time, when circumstances render this necessary or unavoidable; or it will receive and digest, at one meal, a full twenty-four hours supply for the body; or will receive and digest food in small amounts at frequent intervals. The sound stomach, receiving a full tide of nervous energy is a willing and long-suffering servant of the body.

An unsound stomach, that is, one long abused and maltreated by being kept under the perpetual excitement of irritation and stimulation, and by being habitually overworked, will present more and different morbid aspects at different times than it is possible to adequately portray. Its blood vessels become dilated and distended, and, as he abuse continues its coats become thickened and hardened, or, as sometimes occurs, softened. Its glands are impaired. It becomes limited in its digestive power and dietitic-range.

It is unfortunate that, in such a state, the very means that have been employed to bring on this state are the ones that offer the most speedy means of relief. They temporarily mitigate the pain and discomfort only to augment these in the future. The unfortunate victims of their own follies are thus almost irresistably lured on in the increasing repetition of their mistakes. Just as opium relieves the pains it causes only to make them worse, and just as coffee relieves the headache it causes only to fasten the headache upon the victim, so the gluttery of the gourmand will relieve the stomach disorders it causes, only to perpetuate these.

The more stimulating and irritating one's food has been, the more distress and discomfort he experiences during the fast. There may be nausea, vomiting, a gnawing sensation in the stomach, depression, headache, nervousness, etc., all due to the withdrawal of the accustomed stimulation or excitement.

It should be understood that the sick person should give careful attention to the rules and regulations for eating and combining. In fact, it is more necessary for him to do so than for the healthy individual. The healthy person with good digestion may disregard all the rules of diet perhaps for years, without any apparent harm but the sick man with weakened digestion suffers perceptibly following every transgression.

We often hear the young and healthy say "I eat what I please, I do as I like. Nothing hurts me." Our many years of experience in handling the sick and treating all forms of disease have revealed to us the fact that there was a time in the life of nearly every chronic sufferer when he too did and said the same thing. In fact, it often seems that the only trouble they find with their diseased state is that they can no longer eat and do as they once did without suffering. Apparently, the only reason they desire to get well is that they hope to return to the old "flesh pots." It does not seem ever to have entered their minds that their past conduct is responsible for their present woes.

You dear reader, if you now hold to the idea that you may abuse your rugged health and powerful constitution with impunity, should disabuse your mind of this at once. You may be able to digest pig-iron, as you say, but you'll be better off in every way if you do not force yourself to do so. "Don't be a fool just because you happen to know how."

Extreme moderation is required in feeding the sick. If elimination is to proceed with the greatest speed it is necessary that the amount of food eaten be considerably less than that required by the body in health.

All stimulating and irritating foods should be excluded from the diet. All foods that undergo fermentation very readily should be withheld. No denatured foods,—white flour, polished rice, white sugar, degerminated, demineralized corn flour, canned, pickled, embalmed foods, jams, jellies, preserves, pastries, so-called breakfast foods, etc.,—should be consumed. All foods eaten should be wholesome, natural foods. Condiments of every nature should be tabooed.

Such dried fruits as apples, peaches, pears, apricots, fancy dates, figs and raisins are bleeched with sulphurous acid: Crystalized fruit peels, citron, walnuts and almonds are also subjected to this same whitening process. These should never be used, well or sick. The sulphurous acid disturbs metabolism, destroys the blood corpuscles and other cells and over-works the kidneys.

Commercial apple jam and other jams are made up of sulphurated skins and cores. "Chops" as these are called are composed of about 10% fruit, 10% juice. The rest of the jam is composed of about 10% sugar and 70% glucose. The whole is held together and given a jelly like consistency by phosporic acid. Amrath, a coal tar dye, gives it a bright strawberry color while it is prevented from decomposing by benzoate of soda. The government allows one-tenth of one percent of benzoate of soda to be used and requires that it be stated on the lable. It is usually indicated in very fine print. Sulphuric acid is present in almost all commercial syrups and molasses. The syrups have little food value and are harmful in many ways.

The so-called breakfast foods have been refined too much and subjected to such intense heat that their food value is practically all lost.

It can easily be seen that the use of such foods by either the well or sick cannot result in anything else but harm. We have not yet discovered a way to prepare foods, to add to them and subtract from them, that will make them better than they are as Nature gives them to us. Our preparations usually only impair their nutritional value. Until such a method is found it is the part of wisdom for us to stick to the natural foods.

Having decided upon the kind of foods that must be fed the sick—wholesome natural foods, rich in the organic salts and lacking in proteins and carbohydrates—let us now begin our feeding.

It is usually beneficial to begin the treatment of a case of chronic disease with a fast. As fasting will be considered in a separate chapter, we will limit our remarks at this place. The duration of the fast must be determined by the condition and progress of the patient. Usually, such fasts are not necessarily long.

HYGIENE OF CHRONIC DISEASE

The purpose of the fast are manifold. Almost every case of chronic disease is accompanied by a foul gastro-intestinal tract. No health is possible so long as this condition remains. Fasting enables us to get rid of such a condition in the shortest possible time.

It is sometimes found beneficial to precede such a fast with a few days of fresh fruits or raw vegetables. These increase peristalsis and aid in cleansing the intestines and bowels. After the alimentary canal is once thoroughly cleansed and is given a complete rest it will be in a condition to care for the foods eaten in a thoroughly normal manner, whereas before such was not possible.

The length of time that one should fast depends upon the individual's condition. No two cases are alike. A long fast should never be undertaken by any one unacquainted with fasting and ignorant of how to properly conduct it unless under the care of a competent hygienist experienced in handling fasts. Few medical men are capable, because of lack of knowledge and experience with fasting, of conducting a fast. Fasts are always best taken in an institution away from the petty annoyances of friends and relatives.

Feeding after the fast must depend on the individual case. Breaking the fast is a very important matter for if this is not done rightly all the benefits of the fast may be lost. For instructions about how to break the fast see the chapter on fasting.

After the fast is properly broken the best method of feeding the patient consists in placing him or her on a very frugal, cleansing diet of fresh fruits and fresh green leafy vegetables. The patient's weight is purposely kept down by the diet to insure perfect elimination and to insure the absorption of any exudates, deposits, tumerous growth, etc., which were not fully absorbed during the fast.

An acid fruit diet may be employed following a fast of only a few days. This diet may be continued for several days depending on the condition of the patient. Obviously a diet of this kind cannot be employed for more than a few days following an extended fast. Oranges, lemons, grapefruit and acid grapes are the fruits most commonly used. For the conduct of such a diet see chapter on Feeding.

In certain chronic diseases we are brought face to face with the paradoxical proposition that there is but little that can be done and there is much which can be done to restore health.

In liver abscess, fatty degeneration of liver, in cirrhosis (hardening) of the liver, in waxy liver, in cancer of the liver, in cyst of the liver, in ascites, what is there to be done? In Chronic Bright's disease, in degeneration of the kidneys, waxy kidneys, advanced pyelitis, hydronephrois (water on the kidneys) cystic kidneys, tumors and cancers of the kidneys, what can be done? In diabetes, hardening of the arteries, atrophy of the spinal segments, organic heart disease, advanced tuberculosis, etc., what is there that we can do? In arthritis, where the joints are deformed and ankylosed what can be done for such conditions? Other such conditions as these, or rather, the same conditions in other organs, might be named but always with the same question mark after them.

The destroyed parenchyma of the various organs cannot be replaced. The hepatic cells of the liver, renal cells of the kidneys, the destroyed tubules of the kidneys, the islands of Langerhans of the pancreas, the neurons of the spinal cord—these cannot be replaced. The degeneration has reached a stage where regeneration is no longer possible. The hardening cannot be overcome. The overgrowth of connective tissue cannot be removed. Hardened arteries cannot be "softened." The tumor or cancer cannot be cured, except, perhaps, in its earlier stages—and its existence is seldom known in such stages.

In most cases of ascites, what can be done beyond draining off the accumulated fluid at frequent intervals as it continues to accumulate, until the patient dies.

In such cases we deal with seemingly hopeless conditions; conditions which have developed gradually, insiduously, and perhaps with little or no direct warning. This should emphasize the necessity for right living at all times. The mere fact that an individual feels well, looks well, and is able to work and eat is no sufficient proof that his mode of living is not harming him. Indeed he may be on the brink of the grave and imagine himself to be in good health.

As hopeless as such cases appear, and as little as it may appear can be done for them, there is much, very much indeed that we can do and should do. "Cure" will depend on the amount of functioning tissue left. If enough remains to perform the necessary functions of life, and the sufferer will learn to live within the functioning powers of these tissues, he may enjoy good health for many years and the progress of the degenerative condition be stayed. The reader will recall what we learned, in the chapter on *Physiological Compensation,* about the reserve powers of all the organs of man's body. Much of the liver or kidney or pancreas may be destroyed and yet the remaining cells be equal to the work entailed upon them by a normal life or by a life carefully lived. One whole kidney may be removed and, if the other is sound, life and health may continue.

Although the irreparable damages to the organs of the body cannot be undone, if these conditions are discovered early enough, there is much that may be done to stay the further progress of degeneration and decay and to make it possible to live in comfort and a fair degree of health.

The hardening process will be stopt if its causes are corrected. If the causes of degeneration are corrected and removed the process will end. The blood pressure may be lowered to a safe standard and maintained there. The growth of the tumor may be stayed, and, in some cases, materially reduced in size. In liver abscess, the fistula through which it discharges may be caused to heal more rapidly. Comfort may be established and maintained. Life and usefulness may be prolonged. The mode of living may be so ordered and regulated that no undue strain is placed upon the remaining tissues of the impaired organs. If this is done and the invalid will continue to live carefully, that is within his physiological abilities, he may live many years in fair health.

But the true lesson to be derived from the above facts is one of *prevention,* not one of *restoration.* These conditions are all preventable by a correct mode of life. Remember the laws of thy being from thy youth up and you will develop no such conditions. You will have no such problems to meet.